When Change Comes Undone

Management Dilemmas

How often do you wish you could turn to a panel of experts to guide you through tough management situations? The Management Dilemmas series provides just that. Drawn from the pages of *Harvard Business Review*, each insightful volume poses several perplexing predicaments and shares the problem-solving wisdom of leading experts. Engagingly written, these solutions-oriented collections help managers make sound judgment calls when addressing everyday management dilemmas.

Other books in the series

When Good People Behave Badly

When Marketing Becomes a Minefield

MANAGEMENT DILEMMAS

When Change

Comes Undone

Harvard Business School Press

Boston, Massachusetts

The *Harvard Business Review* articles in this collection are available as individual reprints. Discounts apply to quantity purchases. For information and ordering please contact Customer Service, Harvard Business School Publishing, Boston, MA 02163. Telephone (617) 783-7500 or (800) 988-0886, 8 A.M. to 6 P.M. Eastern Time, Monday through Friday. Fax (617) 783-7555, 24 hours a day. E-mail: custserv@hbsp.harvard.edu

Library of Congress Cataloging-in-Publication Data
Management dilemmas. When change comes undone.
        p.   cm. — (Management dilemmas series)
     ISBN 1-59139-503-8
1. Organizational change—Management—Problems, exercises, etc. I.
Title: When change comes undone. II. Harvard Business School Press. III.
Series.
HD58.8.M249 2004
658.4´06—dc22   2004000444

The paper used in this publication meets the minimum requirements of the American National Standard for Information Sciences—Permanence of Paper for Printed Library Materials, ANSI Z39.48-1992.

CONTENTS

Introduction   1

JULIA KIRBY

The Best-Laid Incentive Plans   15

STEVE KERR

Welcome Aboard (But Don't Change a Thing)   45

ERIC MCNULTY

Too Old to Learn?   73

DIANE L. COUTU

The Cost Center That Paid Its Way   101

JULIA KIRBY

Can This Merger Be Saved? 127
SARAH CLIFFE

What's He Waiting For? 157
ROBERT GALFORD

About the Contributors 179

When Change Comes Undone

Introduction

"If you want to make enemies," Woodrow Wilson once observed, "try to change something." He was thinking in terms of political and societal change, but the words ring true for organizational change as well. For as much as commercial enterprises drive change in the world, they are at the end of the day made up of individuals—people with vested interests or at least comfort levels in the status quo.

Almost all veteran executives can tell you a story of a time, early in their careers, when this reality struck them with palpable force. Often it's about the first major project they led, sometimes fresh out of business school. Doing an accurate analysis of the problem was difficult, they will tell you, but enlightening. Designing an elegant solution—whether a new organizational structure, or information system, or way of going to market—was daunting but intellectually stimulating. Getting people to throw their best efforts behind that perfect strategy was—well, an assumption. At best, an afterthought. And, too often, the project's undoing.

It only takes one such experience to teach the first essential lesson about change: It must be carefully managed. Before a plan can come to fruition, the people entrusted with executing it have to believe in it, and they have to understand how it translates to different behaviors and accomplishments at the level of the individual.

But if that first truth can be learned in one lesson, most executives require many more experiences to learn the rest of the truth about transforming an organization. Getting good at change management is much more difficult than recognizing its importance. That's why, at *Harvard Business Review,* we devote so many of our case studies to the subject.

Just-in-Case Advice

Harvard Business Review case studies are uniquely suited to exploring the challenges of change in organizations. The format presents a common managerial dilemma and the advice of several expert commentators on how to resolve it. The dilemma is illustrated by a fictional short story—and therefore overlays questions of business strategy with the often trickier challenges of human emotion and interpersonal dynamics. Nearly always, the commentators are at odds with each other in terms of the solutions they recommend—and that is the point, really. A dilemma wouldn't be a dilemma if all reasonable parties could agree on the path forward.

For the magazine's quarter of a million readers—most of them executives in large organizations—the case goes beyond being a good read. It's a chance for readers to exercise their managerial faculties and to match wits with the experts. Typically, readers study the story line, and then pause to consider what advice they would offer the protagonist. Only then do they go on to read the commentaries, looking for the words of wisdom that align with their own views and expand their perspectives in previously unconsidered ways.

As editors, we try to select topics for cases that are not only intellectually interesting but also broadly relevant. Thus, in this collection, there are cases about change brought about by new leaders, by structural upheavals, by new "rules of the game"—in other words, about the change management issues that confront organizations year in and year out.

Turn and Face the (Strange) Changes

In this collection, we hope you'll find insightful advice to help you manage through your own times of change. So where should you start? You could, of course, begin with the first and read them in order. But a quick overview might help you to select those of greatest interest or relevance to your own organization. Here, title by title, are the key issues raised by the cases and some hints of how the commentators respond:

The Best-Laid Incentive Plans

Steve Kerr, chief learning officer at Goldman Sachs and former head of leadership development at General Electric (responsible for the renowned Crotonville facility), drew the incidents in this case from actual practice in companies he'd studied earlier as a management professor. He had often noted that many companies' compensation schemes, while creating strong incentives to achieve certain outcomes, also brought about unintended consequences. To write this case, we asked Kerr to imagine a company where employees were all too willing to "game the system" to make the numbers required by a new performance management structure. The man behind the metrics is Hiram Phillips, a CFO dreaming of a turnaround in performance. According to his spreadsheets, it's happening. But the reality from managers'—and customers'—points of view looks very different.

Stephen Kaufman, the retired chairman of Arrow Electronics, provides the first commentary on the case, and makes the point that, in performance management, you get what you pay for. The problems in the case might have been avoided, he notes, if Phillips had simply talked to the people who would be affected by his changes, and asked how their behavior would change. Steven Gross of Mercer Human Resources Consulting faults Phillips for focusing on intermediary measures without a big-picture sense of the ultimate goal being served. Gross's own starting point is to ask "What do we want employees to do differently to suppport the business?" and then "Why aren't they already doing it?" Sometimes it's a lack of incentives—but not always. Retired U.S. Navy Admiral Diego Hernández urges management to look beyond pay-for-performance and make more effective use of intangible rewards. Finally, Barry Leskin, former chief learning officer at ChevronTexaco, discusses what it takes to create a strong performance culture: A big part of the challenge is the selection and development of performance-driven leaders.

Welcome Aboard (But Don't Change a Thing)

In this case by Eric McNulty, we see the frustration of Cheryl Hailstrom, the new CEO of Lakeland Wonders. She was recruited to lead the toy company into new growth territory, but doesn't seem to be able to get her head of manufacturing—or design director, or even sales VP—to put their energy and creativity behind her bold new plans. The problem, she believes, is that everyone in the company is too set in their old-fashioned ways. Indeed, the chairman of the company, and head of the family that still owns much of the stock, cautions her that she may need to "pull people along more slowly, to make sure you don't end up tearing the place apart." If only she had that luxury of time. But, as he retired, the scion sold 30% of his holdings to a venture firm, and its leaders are impatient for growth.

Kathleen Calcidise, an executive at Apple Retail Stores, recalls a similar experience of her own in her commentary. "To bring about cultural and performance transformation, I made it the explicit work of several teams. I charged them with identifying any obstacles to change and with recommending new structures, initiatives, and reward systems." A second commentator, executive coach Debra Benton, advises the new CEO to establish "the rules of engagement" with subordinates and to keep them from undermining her decisions. Management consultant Dan Cohen, on the other hand, thinks the CEO in this case has been too assertive. Her driving style, he notes, isn't aligned with the company's culture—and she needs to adjust it. Finally, Nina Aversano, an executive who has worked in a variety of fast-changing organizations, notes a lesson she learned early on: that people support what they create. "You need to engage others in the creation process," she notes, "or you are doomed to failure."

Too Old to Learn?

In "Too Old to Learn?" by HBR Senior Editor Diane Coutu, we see a property and casualty insurance company whose most valuable and senior employees are unequipped to deal with the online revolution in its business. The CEO has hired a new, younger generation of managers to move aggressively onto the Web, but doesn't want to leave his veterans behind; indeed, he believes their knowledge of customer needs must inform the effort. To accomplish that melding of the minds, he pairs up his seniormost eCommerce executive with his most seasoned salesman in a "reverse mentoring" relationship. But the two are at odds from the start, and by the end of the case, the CEO realizes his matchmaking might have lost him a valuable employee.

Monica Higgins, an assistant professor of organizational behavior at Harvard Business School, points out that no change program can succeed simply by imposing a mechanistic mentoring program from above. Mentoring relationships work when they evolve over time, in an informal fashion, through a shared interest in professional development—not when one person is assigned to help another. Lloyd Trotter, EO and president of GE Industrial Systems, reflects on the reverse mentoring program his company has in place—and from which he has personally benefited. He believes Armor Coat can have similarly successful pairings of older and younger employees if the program is repositioned as a tool for collaboration, and if the young people hired are in sync with the company's core values. Psychiatrist and professor Steven Luria Ablon is even more emphatic about the value of learning from mentors, regardless of age. But he notes that the CEO in the case will have to step in and lead by example if this particular relationship is to work. Two managers involved in a reverse mentoring program at Procter & Gamble, Stuart Pearson and Mohan Mohan, identify the problem here as a "huge amount of fear and insecurity in both players," and stress the criticality of mutual deference in a mentoring relationship. Finally, Jerry Wind, a marketing professor at Wharton, says the problems at Armor Coat run even deeper, because the CEO expected to bring about a major change "through the functional silo of technology" without altering anything else about the culture or compensation system. He also notes the folly of placing people who view each other as competitors in a relationship that must have trust at its heart.

The Cost Center That Paid Its Way

In the case study I contributed to this collection, it's a change to organizational structure that's got everyone ruffled. The marketing communications (Mar-Com) group that was once a department—part of the company's overhead expense in the corporate center—has just been converted into a profit center. The logic behind the change is clear, and looks like a win-win situation. The divisions traditionally served by the Mar-Com function will now be treated as valued customers, and charged closer to market rates. The department itself will be able to attract more talented people and get beyond feeling like second-class citizens. Best of all, the new department can take on outside business—and continue to grow, even if the organization around it is downsizing. Why is it that something so wonderful in theory turns out to be generating so many complaints?

The first commentator, Dan Logan, lays the blame at the door of Eric Palmer, the former department head who now has the P&L to run. He's still focusing on boss satisfaction instead of client satisfaction, and needs to transform his mind-set from corporate to entrepreneurial. Logan should know. As head of Trinity Communications, he was in the same position a decade earlier—when New England Financial spun out its marketing department to create his company. Michael McKenney also works in a business that was once a cost center to a larger corporation. To him, Tom O'Reilly, the CEO, is equally to blame in this case for not adequately supporting the business he put in place. But McKenney urges the company to keep the profit center arrangement intact, noting that for his business, doing so has "kept us fresh and competitive." Mark Rice, dean of Babson College and an expert in entrepreneurship, agrees that the positives outweigh the negatives. The way forward is for both executives to acknowledge the problems publicly, understand that they emanate from some flawed assumptions, and come to terms with the trade-offs that will have to be made. Only one commentator, Jeffrey Bennett of Booz Allen

Hamilton questions the wisdom of the profit center model. Many problems would have been avoided, he believes, if the group had been set up as a "shared service" for the company's various businesses—and not for hire by outsiders.

Can This Merger Be Saved?

HBR Executive Editor Sarah Cliffe wrote this case to explore the challenge of cultural assimilation when two large companies come together in a merger or acquisition. Here, the merger is between Synergon Capital, a U.S. financial-services behemoth, and Beauchamp, Becker & Company, a venerable British financial-services company. Before acquiring Beauchamp, Synergon's macho men offered loud assurances that they would leave the tradition-bound company alone—but that was before Beauchamp missed its ambitious target numbers and showed insufficient enthusiasm for cross-selling Synergon's products to its wealthy clients. In charge of making the acquisition work is Nick Cunningham, one of Synergon's more thoughtful executives. Can he bring peace and prosperity to the union?

Acquisition consultant Bill Paul, the first of six commentators on this case, draws an interesting distinction between assimilation and integration. The first is what Synergon has been good at in the past—but it means annihilating the smaller company's culture, which would be catastrophic here. J. Brad McGee, an executive at Tyco, offers a five-point action plan based on the dozens of acquisitions he's been involved in. Jill Greenthal, who was the lead investment banker for TCI in its merger with AT&T, notes the common problem of getting leaders from the acquired firm to stay—and stay productive—after they've been made financially comfortable by the sale. The right deal structure, she says, can help keep them engaged. Dale Matschullat, general counsel at Newell Company, urges Nick Cunningham to focus on getting Beauchamp's managing director to agree on budgetary and strategic goals, and then to leave him in charge of reaching them. But Daniel Vasella, president of Novartis, doubts that Beauchamp's managing director is well suited to growing the business in the way its new parent expects. He would relocate one or two Synergon people, reporting to Synergon's CEO, to accomplish that goal. Finally, Albert Viscio of Booz Allen Hamilton outlines the three elements that have been lacking in this merger: vision, architecture, and leadership. The first step, he says, is for the leaders of both companies to reach a common understanding of how this merger will add strategic value.

What's He Waiting For?

Robert Galford's case presents an interesting counterpoint to the other cases in this volume. Here, the problem isn't one of too much change, but too little. It's been nearly a year since Doug Yacubian joined Captiva Corporation as its first-ever COO, with much fanfare about the entrepreneurial spirit and operational discipline he would bring to the century-old company. But in that time, he's managed to make very little impact. The rest of Captiva's leadership team is left to wonder whether the cause of the problem is a non-starter of a hire—or a CEO who can't bring himself to delegate. Can one of them—namely division president Cynthia Speedwell—figure out how to get the company moving forward?

Miki Tsusaka of the Boston Consulting Group, thinks Speedwell can make a difference; in fact, she outlines a five-point plan the executive can use to get her bosses back on track. One important component is to have the CEO and COO draw up a list of tangible goals they are jointly committed to, and communicate them to the company. Mark Smith, however, says the burden must fall on the COO to find a way to add more value. As a managing director at executive search firm Korn/Ferry, his perspective is that the COO might have made a serious career blunder by getting into a position where he was in over his head. Fred Foulkes, a management professor at Boston University, suggests that an executive coach might be valuable in this situation. At the very least, the COO needs to have a heart-to-heart with his boss. George Hornig, formerly an executive at Deutsche Bank, concurs. He notes how critical it is, when a new number two comes in from outside, to build a strong relationship with the CEO. But he places more of the blame on the CEO himself, for not relinquishing more responsibility.

The Only Constant Is Change

Six cases certainly don't exhaust the possibilities of how change can tear the fabric of an organization—or the ways in which managers can respond. But after reading and reflecting on these six, you should find yourself better equipped to deal with any number of change management challenges.

Think of a case study as a way to exercise basic managerial faculties—which can then be applied to many situations. Professional education, in general, is about learning to deal with problems that require diagnosis and treatment. It involves learning rules and standards, but also developing good judgment. Architects who lack experience gain it through simulations. Surgeons practice on cadavers. Emergency workers hone their reflexes through drills. For managers, the equivalent is the case study. No question, it is only a partial reflection of the real complexity and trauma involved in real-world change. And no question, actual experience remains the best teacher. But it's also true that you will learn more from reflecting on a case study than on living through a real change without reflecting on its lessons.

One way or another, if you are to succeed as a manager, you will need to become adept at managing change. Peter Drucker explains it this way: "Society, community, family are all conserving institutions. They try to maintain stability, and to prevent, or at least to slow down, change. But the organization of the post-capitalist society of organizations is a destabilizer. Because its function is to put knowledge to work—on tools, processes, and products; on work; on knowledge itself—it must be organized for constant change."

The corollary, of course, is that the work of managers—the markets they serve, the organizations they work in, the tools they use—will never stop evolving. But one thing will never change: their need to get better at change management.

The Best-Laid

Incentive Plans

Executive Summary

Hiram Phillips couldn't have been in better spirits. The CFO and chief administrative officer of Rainbarrel Products, a diversified consumer-durables manufacturer, Phillips felt he'd single-handedly turned the company's performance around. He'd only been at Rainbarrel a year, but the company's numbers had, according to his measures, already improved by leaps and bounds.

Now the day has come for Hiram to share the positive results of his new performance management system with his colleagues. The corporate executive council was meeting, and even CEO Keith Randall was applauding the CFO's work: "Hiram's going to give us some very good news about cost reductions and operating efficiencies, all due to the changes he's designed and implemented this year." Everything looked positively rosy—until some questionable information began to trickle in from other meeting participants.

It came to light, for instance, that R&D had developed a breakthrough product that was not being brought to market as quickly as it should have been—thanks to Hiram's inflexible budgeting process. Then, too, an employee survey showed that workers were demoralized. And customers were complaining about Rainbarrel's service. The general message? The new performance metrics and incentives had indeed been affecting overall performance—but not for the better.

Should Rainbarrel revisit its approach to performance management? Commentators Stephen Kaufman, a senior lecturer at Harvard Business School; compensation consultant Steven Gross; retired U.S. Navy vice admiral and management consultant Diego Hernández; and Barry Leskin, a consultant and former chief learning officer for Chevron Texaco, offer their advice in this fictional case study.

Hiram Phillips finished tying his bow tie and glanced in the mirror. Frowning, he tugged on the left side, then caught sight of his watch in the mirror. Time to get going. Moments later, he was down the stairs, whistling cheerfully and heading toward the coffeemaker.

"You're in a good mood," his wife said, looking up from the newspaper and smiling. "What's that tune? 'Accentuate the Positive'?"

"Well done!" Hiram called out. "You know, I do believe you're picking up some pop culture in spite of yourself." It was a running joke with them. She was a classically trained cellist and on the board of the local symphony. He was the one with the Sinatra and Bing Crosby albums and the taste for standards. "You're getting better at naming that tune."

"Or else you're getting better at whistling." She looked over her reading glasses and met his eye. They let a beat pass before they said in unison: "Naaah." Then, with a wink, Hiram shrugged on his trench coat, grabbed his travel mug, and went out the door.

Fat and Happy

It was true. Hiram Phillips, CFO and chief administrative officer of Rainbarrel Products, a diversified consumer-durables manufacturer, was in a particularly good mood. He was heading into a breakfast meeting that would bring nothing but good news. Sally Hamilton and Frank Ormondy from Felding & Company would no doubt already be at the office when he arrived and would have with them the all-important numbers—the statistics that would demonstrate the positive results of the performance management system he'd put in place a year ago. Hiram had already seen many of the figures in bits and pieces. He'd retained the consultants to establish baselines on the metrics he wanted to watch and had seen various interim reports from them since. But today's meeting would be the impressive summation capping off a year's worth of effort. Merging into the congestion of Route 45, he thought about the upbeat presentation he would spend the rest of the morning preparing for tomorrow's meeting of the corporate executive council.

It was obvious enough what his introduction should be. He would start at the beginning—or, anyway, his own beginning at Rainbarrel Products a year ago. At the time, the company had just come off a couple of awful quarters. It wasn't alone. The sudden slowdown in consumer spending, after a decade-long boom, had taken the whole industry by surprise. But what had quickly become clear was that Rainbarrel was adjusting to the new reality far less rapidly than its biggest competitors.

Keith Randall, CEO of Rainbarrel, was known for being an inspiring leader who focused on innovation. Even outside the industry, he had a name as a marketing visionary. But over the course of the ten-year economic boom, he had allowed his organization to become a little lax.

Take corporate budgeting. Hiram still smiled when he recalled his first day of interviews with Rainbarrel's executives. It immediately became obvious that the place had no budget integrity whatsoever. One unit head had said outright, "Look, none of us fights very hard at budget time, because after three or four months, nobody looks at the budget anyway." Barely concealing his shock, Hiram asked how that could be; what did they look at, then? The answer was that they operated according to one simple rule: "If it's a good idea, we say yes to it. If it's a bad idea, we say no."

"And what happens," Hiram had pressed, "when you run out of money halfway through the year?" The fellow rubbed his chin and took a moment to think before answering. "I guess we've always run out of good ideas before we've run out of money." Unbelievable!

"Fat and happy" was how Hiram characterized Rainbarrel in a conversation with the headhunter who had recruited him. Of course, he wouldn't use those words in the CEC meeting. That would sound too disparaging. In fact, he'd quickly fallen in love with Rainbarrel and the opportunities it presented. Here was a company that had the potential for greatness but that was held back by a lack of discipline. It was like a racehorse that had the potential to be a Secretariat but lacked a structured training regimen. Or a Ferrari engine that needed the touch of an expert mechanic to get it back in trim. In other words, the only thing Rainbarrel was missing was what someone like Hiram Phillips could bring to the table. The allure was irresistible; this was the assignment that would define his career. And now, a year later, he was ready to declare a turnaround.

Lean and Mean

Sure enough, as Hiram steered toward the entrance to the parking garage, he saw Sally and Frank in a visitor parking space, pulling their bulky file bags out of the trunk of Sally's sedan. He caught up to them at the security checkpoint in the lobby and took a heavy satchel from Sally's hand.

Moments later, they were at a conference table, each of them poring over a copy of the consultants' spiral-bound report. "This is great," Hiram said. "I can hand this out just as it is. But what I want to do while you're here is to really nail down what the highlights are. I have the floor for 40 minutes, but I guess I'd better leave ten for questions. There's no way I can plow through all of this."

"If I were you," Sally advised, "I would lead off with the best numbers. I mean, none of them are bad. You hit practically every target. But some of these, where you even exceeded the stretch goal . . ."

Hiram glanced at the line Sally was underscoring with her fingernail. It was an impressive achievement: a reduction in labor costs. This had been one of the first moves he'd made, and he'd tried to do it gently. He came up with the idea of identifying the bottom quartile of performers throughout the company and offering them fairly generous buyout packages. But when that hadn't attracted enough takers, he'd gone the surer route. He imposed an across-the-board headcount reduction of 10% on all the units. In that round, the affected people were given no financial assistance beyond the normal severance.

"It made a big difference," he nodded. "But it wasn't exactly the world's most popular move." Hiram was well aware that a certain segment of the Rainbarrel workforce currently referred to him as "Fire 'em." He pointed to another number on the spreadsheet. "Now, that one tells a happier story: lower costs as a result of higher productivity."

"And better customer service to boot," Frank chimed in. They were talking about the transformation of Rainbarrel's call center—where phone representatives took orders and handled questions and complaints from both trade and retail customers. The spreadsheet indicated a dramatic uptick in productivity: The number of calls each service rep was handling per day had gone up 50%. A year earlier, reps were spending up to six minutes per call, whereas now the average was less than four minutes. "I guess you decided to go for that new automated switching system?" Frank asked.

"No!" Hiram answered. "That's the beauty of it. We got that improvement without any capital investment. You know what we did? We just announced the new targets, let everyone know we were going to monitor them, and put the names of the worst offenders on a great big 'wall of shame' right outside the cafeteria. Never underestimate the power of peer pressure!"

Sally, meanwhile, was already circling another banner achievement: an increase in on-time shipments. "You should talk about this, given that it's something that wasn't even being watched before you came."

It was true. As much as Rainbarrel liked to emphasize customer service in its values and mission statement, no reliable metric had been in place to track it. And getting a metric in place hadn't been as straightforward as it might seem—people haggled about what constituted "on time" and even what constituted "shipped." Finally, Hiram had put his foot down and insisted on the most objective of measures. On time meant when the goods were promised to ship. And nothing was counted as shipped till it left company property. Period. "And once again," Hiram announced, "not a dollar of capital expenditure. I simply let people know that, from now on, if they made commitments and didn't keep them, we'd have their number."

"Seems to have done the trick," Sally observed. "The percentage of goods shipped by promise date has gone up steadily for the last six months. It's now at 92%."

Scanning the report, Hiram noticed another huge percentage gain, but he couldn't recall what the acronym stood for. "What's this? Looks like a good one: a 50% cost reduction?"

Sally studied the item. "Oh, that. It's pretty small change, actually. Remember we separated out the commissions on sales to employees?" It came back to Hiram immediately. Rainbarrel had a policy that allowed current and retired employees to buy products at a substantial discount. But the salespeople who served them earned commissions based on the full retail value, not the actual price paid. So, in effect, employee purchases were jacking up the commission expenses. Hiram had created a new policy in which the commission reflected the actual purchase price. On its own, the change didn't amount to a lot, but it reminded Hiram of a larger point he wanted to make in his presentation: the importance of straightforward rules—and rewards—in driving superior performance.

"I know you guys don't have impact data for me, but I'm definitely going to talk about the changes to commission structure and sales incentives. There's no question they must be making a difference."

"Right," Sally nodded. "A classic case of 'keep it simple,' isn't it?" She turned to Frank to explain. "The old way they calculated commissions was by using this really complicated formula that factored in, I can't remember, at least five different things."

"Including sales, I hope?" Frank smirked.

"I'm still not sure!" Hiram answered. "No, seriously, sales were the most important single variable, but they also mixed in all kinds of targets around mentoring, prospecting new clients, even keeping the account information current. It was all way too subjective, and salespeople were getting very mixed signals. I just clarified the message so they don't have to wonder what they're getting paid for. Same with the sales contests. It's simple now: If you sell the most product in a given quarter, you win."

With Sally and Frank nodding enthusiastically, Hiram again looked down at the report. Row after row of numbers attested to Rainbarrel's improved performance. It wouldn't be easy to choose the rest of the high lights, but what a problem to have! He invited the consultants to weigh in again and leaned back to bask in the superlatives. And his smile grew wider.

Cause for Concern

The next morning, a well-rested Hiram Phillips strode into the building, flashed his ID badge at Charlie, the guard, and joined the throng in the lobby. In the crowd waiting for the elevator, he recognized two young women from Rainbarrel, lattes in hand and head-phones around their necks. One was grimacing melo-dramatically as she turned to her friend. "I'm so dread-ing getting to my desk," she said. "Right when I was leaving last night, an e-mail showed up from the buyer at Sullivan. I just know it's going to be some big, hairy problem to sort out. I couldn't bring myself to open it, with the day I'd had. But I'm going to be sweating it today trying to respond by five o'clock. I can't rack up any more late responses, or my bonus is seriously his-tory."

Her friend had slung her backpack onto the floor and was rooting through it, barely listening. But she glanced up to set her friend straight in the most casual way. "No, see, all they check is whether you responded to an e-mail within 24 hours of opening it. So that's the key. Just don't open it. You know, till you've got time to deal with it."

Then a belltone announced the arrival of the eleva-tor, and they were gone.

More Cause for Concern

An hour later, Keith Randall was calling to order the quarterly meeting of the corporate executive council. First, he said, the group would hear the results of the annual employee survey, courtesy of human resources VP Lew Hart. Next would come a demonstration by the chief marketing officer of a practice the CEO hoped to incorporate into all future meetings. It was a "quick market intelligence," or QMI, scan, engaging a few of Rainbarrel's valued customers in a prearranged—but not predigested—conference call, to collect raw data on customer service concerns and ideas. "And finally," Keith concluded, "Hiram's going to give us some very good news about cost reductions and operating efficiencies, all due to the changes he's designed and implemented this past year."

Hiram nodded to acknowledge the compliment. He heard little of the next ten minutes' proceedings, thinking instead about how he should phrase certain points for maximum effect. Lew Hart had lost him in the first moments of his presentation on the "people survey" by beginning with an overview of "purpose, methodology, and historical trends." Deadly.

It was the phrase "mindlessly counting patents" that finally turned Hiram's attention back to his colleague. Lew, it seemed, was now into the "findings" section of his remarks. Hiram pieced together that he was reporting on an unprecedented level of negativity in the responses from Rainbarrel's R&D department and was quoting the complaints people had scribbled on their surveys. "Another one put it this way," Lew said. "We're now highly focused on who's getting the most patents, who's getting the most copyrights, who's submitting the most grant proposals, etc. But are we more creative? It's not that simple."

"You know," Rainbarrel's chief counsel noted, "I have thought lately that we're filing for a lot of patents for products that will never be commercially viable."

"But the thing that's really got these guys frustrated seems to be their 'Innovation X' project," Lew continued. "They're all saying it's the best thing since sliced bread, a generational leap on the product line, but they're getting no uptake."

Eyes in the room turned to the products division president, who promptly threw up his hands. "What can I say, gang? We never expected that breakthrough to happen in this fiscal year. It's not in the budget to bring it to market."

Lew Hart silenced the rising voices, reminding the group he had more findings to share. Unfortunately, it didn't get much better. Both current and retired employees were complaining about being treated poorly by sales personnel when they sought to place orders or obtain information about company products. There was a lot of residual unhappiness about the layoffs, and not simply because those who remained had more work to do. Some people had noted that, because the reduction was based on headcount, not costs, managers had tended to fire low-level people, crippling the company without saving much money. And because the reduction was across the board, the highest performing departments had been forced to lay off some of the company's best employees. Others had heard about inequities in the severance deals: "As far as I can tell, we gave our lowest performers a better package than our good ones," he quoted one employee as saying.

And then there was a chorus of complaints from the sales organization. "No role models." "No mentoring." "No chance to pick the veterans' brains." "No knowledge sharing about accounts." More than ever, salespeople were dissatisfied with their territories and clamoring for the more affluent, high-volume districts. "It didn't help that all the sales-contest winners this year were from places like Scarsdale, Shaker Heights, and Beverly Hills," a salesperson was quoted as saying. Lew concluded with a promise to look further into the apparent decline in morale to determine whether it was an aberration.

The Ugly Truth

But if the group thought the mood would improve in the meeting's next segment—the QMI chat with the folks at longtime customer Brenton Brothers—they soon found out otherwise. Booming out of the speakerphone in the middle of the table came the Southern-tinged voices of Billy Brenton and three of his employees representing various parts of his organization.

"What's up with your shipping department?" Billy called out. "My people are telling me it's taking forever to get the stock replenished."

Hiram sat up straight, then leaned toward the speakerphone. "Excuse me, Mr. Brenton. This is Hiram

Phillips—I don't believe we've met. But are you saying we are not shipping by our promise date?"

A cough—or was it a guffaw?—came back across the wire. "Well, son. Let me tell you about that. First of all, what y'all promise is not always what we are saying we require—and what we believe we deserve. Annie, isn't that right?"

"Yes, Mr. Brenton," said the buyer. "In some cases, I've been told to take a late date or otherwise forgo the purchase. That becomes the promise date, I guess, but it's not the date I asked for."

"And second," Billy continued, "I can't figure out how you fellas define 'shipped.' We were told last Tuesday an order had been shipped, and come to find out, the stuff was sitting on a railroad siding across the street from your plant."

"That's an important order for us," another Brenton voice piped up. "I sent an e-mail to try to sort it out, but I haven't heard back about it." Hiram winced, recalling the conversation in the lobby that morning. The voice persisted: "I thought that might be the better way to contact your service people these days? They always seem in such an all-fired hurry to get off the phone when I call. Sometimes it takes two or three calls to get something squared away."

The call didn't end there—a few more shortcomings were discussed. Then Keith Randall, to his credit, pulled the conversation onto more positive ground by reaffirming the great regard Rainbarrel had for Brenton

Brothers and the mutual value of that enduring relationship. Promises were made and hearty thanks extended for the frank feedback. Meanwhile, Hiram felt the eyes of his colleagues on him. Finally, the call ended and the CEO announced that he, for one, needed a break before the last agenda item.

Dazed and Confused

Hiram considered following his boss out of the room and asking him to table the whole discussion of the new metrics and incentives. The climate was suddenly bad for the news he had looked forward to sharing. But he knew that delaying the discussion would be weak and wrong. After all, he had plenty of evidence to show he was on the right track. The problems the group had just been hearing about were side effects, but surely they didn't outweigh the cure.

He moved to the side table and poured a glass of ice water, then leaned against the wall to collect his thoughts. Perhaps he should reframe his opening comments in light of the employee and customer feedback. As he considered how he might do so, Keith Randall appeared at his side.

"Looks like we have our work cut out for us, eh Hiram?" he said quietly—and charitably enough. "Some of those metrics taking hold, um, a little too strongly?" Hiram started to object but saw the seriousness in his boss's eyes.

He lifted the stack of reports Felding & Company had prepared for him and turned to the conference table. "Well, I guess that's something for the group to talk about."

Should Rainbarrel Revisit Its Approach to Performance Management?

Four commentators offer expert advice.

➤ Stephen P. Kaufman

Stephen P. Kaufman recently retired as chairman of the board of Arrow Electronics, a company he served as CEO for 14 years. He is a senior lecturer at Harvard Business School in Boston.

If Rainbarrel were within a month of bankruptcy and in the hands of a turnaround manager, the kinds of changes Hiram has imposed wouldn't be so unusual and might even be considered reasonable. But as far as I can tell, Rainbarrel just needs to tighten its belt in a period of cyclically soft sales and more aggressive competition. The case portrays Rainbarrel Products as a basically healthy and successful company.

But I'd bet that we as readers are seeing only half the trouble Hiram has caused. Given the pressure to ship faster, the warehouse is probably making more errors and thus adding to the number of returns and customer complaints.

Now that every department has cut its staff, the company is probably hiring more expensive temps, consultants, and outsourcing firms. And let's not even speculate on what the impact of a "wall of shame" might be. That's the kind of humiliating tactic that could turn a devoted employee into a saboteur.

These troubles should be enough to teach Rainbarrel the first rule of performance management: You get what you pay for. If the warehouse workers are praised for putting a box over an imaginary line, they will put it there even if it's not ready. If you pay the sales force only for sales dollars, you might end up with more sales, but at bad prices or with too many extra services promised. I remember a time at Arrow Electronics when we decided to pay out a part of the sales reps' commissions at the time they took the customers' orders. The result was that we got orders that never shipped—or that were shipped and later returned for full credit. One veteran salesman explained it this way, and I've heard the phrase many times since: "Look, you make the rules, we'll play the game."

Before top management starts introducing new rules, then, it had better have a good sense of the kinds of games these rules may promote. Hiram is blindsided by the discovery that his customer service people have learned not to open problematic e-mails. I made a similar mistake years ago by requiring Arrow warehouses to ship all orders received by 4 PM the same day. Since the orders were routed by our computer to a printer in the warehouse, the key to

100% same-day shipping performance was obvious: They pulled the plug on the printer at three o'clock.

All of this suggests another truism about performance management: The devil is in the details. It's very difficult to define the right metric and anticipate exactly how your people will react to it. Your best chance of knowing whether it will have the intended effect is to talk to the people directly involved as well as their immediate supervisors. It's very telling that Hiram is seen meeting with only his henchmen. He needs to go to the cafeteria, get a tray, and sit with the people who are doing the work at Rainbarrel. If he were my new chief financial officer, I'd have told him, "Staple yourself to the back of a warehouse manager for a week. Take the time to follow a general manager around his division. Ride along with some salespeople. Spend several months getting to know this company really well before you settle into your staff job." Hiram knows nothing about Rainbarrel's industry and how it works and knows little or nothing about the culture of the company. He must understand both in order to know what kind and what pace of change are appropriate in this situation.

That point brings me to a big question about the Rainbarrel case. Where has the CEO been? Keith Randall has seriously abdicated his responsibilities as chief executive in giving a newly hired CFO such free rein—and across such a broad range of functions, many of them typically not a CFO's job. When I was a young man, my father told me, "Good judgment comes from experience. But unfortunately, experience comes from bad judgment." A manager's career is all about building a base of good judgment on the back of mistakes. Hiram, if he's at all reflective, will learn a lesson here. But his boss should have known it by now.

➢ Steven E. Gross

Steven E. Gross leads the U.S. compensation consulting practice of Mercer Human Resource Consulting. Based in Philadelphia, he is a frequent author and speaker on reward issues.

The good news in this case is that we see a senior management team that is focusing on performance measures as a way of creating more accountability for results. The bad news is that the team is using the wrong measures, and it has gone about establishing them in the wrong way. As a result, it is sacrificing long-term business success for short-term operational gains. What Rainbarrel needs are performance metrics that are less employee focused and more customer focused. But even these kinds of externally focused measures are likely to be ineffective unless management can successfully help workers understand and accept them.

The only reasonable way to embark on any performance management effort is to define the criteria for success, and that's a step Hiram seems to have skipped. What's the ultimate goal? Sales? Profits? Retained business? Lacking that big picture, Hiram is focusing on intermediary steps and assuming that such enhancements will produce a positive impact on the bottom line. Measuring the number of calls being handled by the call center is a good example. That's a customer service measure but not an indicator of customer satisfaction. "Did one call solve the customer's problem?" might be a better question for them to ask. Employee turnover is another metric that might make sense, given that employee tenure is highly correlated to the quality of customer service in these kinds of jobs. Practically speaking, it's always tricky to balance what can be measured objectively and internally, what customers really want, and what ultimately creates value for the organization.

If I were Hiram, I wouldn't have made a single change until I'd asked two basic questions: "What do we want employees to do differently to support the business?" and "Why aren't they already doing it?" The answers to the second question will yield the greatest insights. Is it that they don't have the knowledge or skills? Or is it that they don't have sufficient tools or infrastructure? Is it a question of motivation? And if it's a question of motivation, do people need to be spurred to work harder or smarter? Many of Hiram's metrics were based on the assumption that the organization wasn't working hard enough, but that's usually not the case in most companies. Overwhelmingly, I think, people want to do a good job. Has anyone asked the warehouse workers why some orders weren't being delivered on time?

There is no evidence that Hiram sought any input from employees on the design of his measures, and I suspect that his approach to rolling out the new program featured information versus communication and education. If he wanted buy-in from employees, he should have gone much further than simply telling them what their goals were, helping them instead to genuinely understand why those objectives mattered to the business and to shareholders. He should have launched his program as a pilot and made it clear to employees that it would be refined based on their experience and input.

Even better, at the outset, he could have explained the company's goals and then let employees own the process of defining how the goals should be reached and how progress toward them should be measured. I remember a time I was advising a client who ran a mine in Wyoming. Management wanted to bring down costs and had placed incentives for savings on all the factors that influenced costs. The company found itself paying out bonuses, yet the profitability of the mine didn't improve. We were asked to investigate, and since the quantitative results were inconclusive, we went to Wyoming for some qualitative feedback. We asked the workers, "Is there anything you've done in the past 12 months that you might not have done if not for the bonus plan?" There was: They had shut off some of the faucets to conserve water. The problem was, less water flow meant less throughput of the material they were extracting. So, yes, water conservation yielded a 12% improvement on that metric. But the ultimate outcome was that the operation made less money due to lower productivity.

This is a perfect example of how you become what you reward. By rewarding the wrong short-term performance, this company was missing the greater opportunity for long-term success.

➤ Vice Admiral Diego E. Hernández

Vice Admiral Diego E. Hernández (U.S. Navy, retired) is a management consultant in both the public and private sectors and serves on a number of corporate boards. He is based in Miami Lakes, Florida.

Let's spend a moment assessing Hiram's job performance over the past year. In that short period of time, he has managed to create a climate of uncertainty and self-preservation among employees by reducing the workforce in two poorly planned increments. He has eliminated workers without reducing the amount of work. He has established the wrong metrics for customer service, shipping, and R&D. He has arrested the development of the company's next generation of salespeople. He has delayed the launch of a breakthrough product. He has publicly humiliated company employees. And he has succeeded in teaching Rainbarrel's workers that the best use of their time and energy is in devising ways to game the system.

Yes, I would say that Hiram needs to rethink his approach.

But I would hasten to add that Rainbarrel's problems don't begin and end with the CFO and his performance metrics. He is clearly oblivious to what his actions have done to the company, but he is not the only one. The CEO, first and foremost, doesn't seem to be paying attention to his people or his customers. The VP of human resources says he doesn't know what to make of the apparent decline in morale. The products division president knew he had a product breakthrough that was not funded but did not raise the issue with the CEO. The chief counsel knew that many of the patents he was reviewing were not commercially viable. There is something fundamentally wrong in a company where executives do not communicate openly and continually with one another about the business— where they do not question questionable things. Is it any surprise that rank-and-file employees aren't sufficiently focused on what is good for the company? Their leaders obviously aren't.

Effective performance management begins with clear two-way communications to ensure goals are understood and accepted. Even more, it requires multiple feedback channels for employees so that they can inform managers of any problem areas in their jobs. Senior managers cannot make good decisions without knowing the truth, and at Rainbarrel, they aren't hearing it.

When it comes to improving individual performance, I would urge Rainbarrel's management to look beyond pay for performance and make more effective use of intangible rewards. Public recognition, a letter of appreciation, or a word of praise can do a great deal to focus an individual's attention on organizational targets. Such motivational tools are powerful yet terribly underused in business settings.

That bias comes from my naval experience, no doubt. Leaders in the U.S. armed services have no control over compensation levels and don't have the option of giving bonuses to high performers. We're intensely focused on mission achievement and realize that's entirely dependent on everyone buying in and giving it everything they've got—but the pay scales are set by Congress. How do we motivate people? We set high goals and communicate them simply and repeatedly. We take pains to establish valid metrics. We provide the means for people to achieve those goals, and we help remove the obstacles that always arise. In order to do that, we listen to people's concerns and make use of multiple feedback loops so we can hear the truth. We create interim goals and publicly recognize interim successes. We differentiate, with an aim to promoting the top performers and getting rid of underperformers. And we do all this continuously. In the end, our people identify strongly with the goals of the organization and feel energized when they achieve these goals. And I can testify that there is nothing more electrifying to a leader than obtaining that level of commitment.

Right now, Rainbarrel's management is witnessing the opposite condition. Employees are thoroughly alienated, for good reason, and they will have to reconnect with the company before anything good can happen. Management's immediate focus should be to create the conditions that will allow employees to achieve Rainbarrel's goals and to find ways to acknowledge and reward those achievements.

Metrics are important, but the key to high performance is within people.

➤ Barry Leskin

Barry Leskin was the chief learning officer for ChevronTexaco, the human resources partner at Ernst & Young, UK, and the chairman of the management and organization department at the University of Southern California's Marshall School of Business. He is now an independent consultant.

Unfortunately for Rainbarrel, it needs to spend some time undoing the damage done by Hiram Phillips. As soon as possible, the CEO should focus on two change strategies for short-term and systemwide performance improvement: selecting performance-driven leaders and aligning the performance culture with the company's strategic direction.

Research has demonstrated that a company's top performers in mid- to senior-level jobs have a tremendous effect on corporate outcomes—that is, these top performers are 50% more productive than their average-performing counterparts. That means it's imperative to identify and develop these significant contributors early on, ensure that they have the right skills, and then place them in high-level positions. Doing so may be one of the most effective ways to build and sustain a strong performance culture and, in turn, improve performance.

That said, creating a strong performance culture isn't enough to change overall performance. A company must also align its performance and reward culture with its strategies. Indeed, a well-communicated strategy, with an integrated set of activities to support it, can itself signal to employees what senior executives really value, even if the leaders are advocating one set of behaviors and unintentionally rewarding another. But a company achieves its greatest advantage when performance culture and strategy reinforce each other and senior leaders consistently reward the activities they advocate.

Selecting the right leaders and aligning culture with strategy, though critical to performance, are considered by some to be "soft" initiatives, and their importance may be underestimated by leaders who focus mainly on results. Such leaders are apt to continually seek engineering solutions to people issues—to no avail.

Hiram seems to fit this description. He has introduced performance metrics without thinking them through or consulting other business-unit heads about how these changes will affect the company. He has actually hurt performance. And Keith Randall isn't any better. After all, he chose Hiram as a leader. What does this tell you about his understanding of how to lead organizational change? What signal has he sent to employees about his criteria for selecting senior leaders, and how does this affect his credibility?

During my career as a consultant and HR executive, I've seen many companies like Rainbarrel that unintentionally discourage employee behaviors that might increase corporate performance. For instance, top executives at one company tried to measure individuals' performance and leadership skills by asking in a 360-degree survey "to what extent the leader provides consequences to those who commit to performance contracts and miss them." The problem was, high scores on this item, meaning the leader was likely to provide consequences, had a low correlation with "effective leadership" in the survey. In other words, those who provided consequences were less likely to be seen as competent leaders by subordinates and peers. So in effect, the company was signaling that it valued relationships and harmony over results.

Many companies also discourage behaviors like challenging the status quo and raising difficult issues, which are essential to corporate performance. When candidates who display these behaviors are up for high-level positions, they often lose out because they're considered rebellious or in need of "polish."

Just as illogical is the way that pay-for-performance plays out in most companies. The whole point of such schemes is to differentiate and improve individual performance. But since employees know their target bonus, and the bonus pools are zero-sum, it's impossible for a manager to give one individual an outsize reward without penalizing one or more average performers, however slightly. Faced with this outcome, managers routinely default to the same target for everyone, fearful of demotivating the average performers. And that reluctance undermines all the power of performance-based pay, effectively punishing the high performers.

I could offer up more in this vein, but my point is simple. If Keith Randall selects the right leaders, communicates a clear set of goals, and aligns the company's performance culture with its strategy, results will be achieved—slowly in the short term, perhaps, but exponentially faster over time.

Originally published in January 2003

Reprint R0301A

Welcome Aboard

(But Don't Change a Thing)

Executive Summary

Cheryl Hailstrom, the CEO of Lakeland Wonders, a manufacturer of high-quality wooden toys, is the first person outside the Swensen family to hold the top job. But she's not a stranger to this 94-year-old company: She'd been the COO of one of its largest customers and had worked with Lakeland to develop many best-selling products. Wally Swensen IV, the previous CEO, chose Cheryl because she knew how to generate profits and because he believed her energy and enthusiasm could take the company to the next level.

Yet here she is, nearing her six-month anniversary, wondering why her expansive vision for the company isn't taking hold. She's tried to lead by example: traveling a pounding schedule to visit customers, setting aggressive project deadlines, and proposing a bonus schedule. She has a plan to reach the board's growth goals—going beyond Lakeland's core upscale market and launching into the midmarket with an exclusive toy contract with a new customer.

The problem is that while Cheryl's senior managers are giving her the nod on the surface, they're all really dragging their feet. Some fear that offshore outsourcing will hurt their brand, not to mention make for tricky union negotiations. Others are balking at trying a new design firm.

Is Cheryl pushing too much change too quickly? Should she bring in outsiders to seedily adopt the changes she envisions and overhaul Lakeland's corporate culture? Or should she keep trying to work with the current team? Commentators Kathleen Calcidise of Apple Retail Stores; executive coach Debra Benton; Dan Cohen, coauthor of *The Heart of Change*; and consultant Nina Aversano offer advice in this fictional case study.

Cheryl Hailstrom checked her wristwatch as she made her way toward the office of Mark Dawson, her senior vice president of operations. It was only 6:30 PM, but the building seemed deserted. "That's another thing that's going to have to change if we're going to make it in the twenty-first century," she muttered to herself. The thick report she carried—the one on manufacturing strategy that Mark had prepared—weighed heavily on her mind. It was clear that Mark had no intention of moving quickly to make her vision of the company a reality. He didn't even seem to understand that vision, much less buy in to it. But she had waited long enough. The time had come to set him straight—if, that is, he hadn't already bolted for home like everyone else.

Cheryl was just approaching her six-month anniversary as the CEO of Lakeland Wonders. A manufacturer of high-quality wooden toys, it had three plants in Minnesota and almost 5,000 employees. Brought in when Walter Swensen IV was ready to retire and it was clear that none of his children wanted to take an active role in the business, she was the first person from outside the family to hold the top job. But she wasn't entirely a newcomer. Her relationship with the company had started years earlier when she was the general merchandise manager, and later the COO, of one of Lakeland's largest customers, Kids&Company, an upscale retail chain based in Chicago. Cheryl had worked with Lakeland to develop new products for which Kids&Company had six-month exclusives; many of those became best-sellers.

Cheryl was widely known as the driving force behind the growth of Kids&Company from a small regional chain to a national presence with more than 150 stores. Her energy and enthusiasm were infectious, and she always seemed to be one step ahead of the market. Most important, she knew how to generate profits. Swensen saw her as the logical succession choice, and he spent several months persuading her to take the reins. He wanted Lakeland to grow, and he felt sure Cheryl would take this 94-year-old company to the next level. After all, even though he was stepping down, his holdings in the company were still the primary source of wealth for him and his family.

Now, as she strode toward Mark's office, Cheryl wondered why her expansive vision for Lakeland didn't seem to be taking hold. She tried to lead by example: traveling a pounding schedule to visit customers, setting aggressive deadlines for new projects, and proposing a bonus scheme to the union for improving cycle times. But the sales force was only slowly increasing the number of calls it was making without her, and her bonus plan had been received indifferently by the union officials. They'd be happy to produce more, they said, but only if Cheryl agreed to put on a third shift. Mark's lukewarm report on offshore manufacturing was just the latest hitch. It seemed as though her managers were giving her the nod on the surface, all the while building elaborate arguments for going more slowly than she knew they needed to go.

She came through the doorway as Mark was shutting down his computer. "Got a minute?" she asked.

Mark leaned back in his chair with a hint of resignation. "Sure, boss." He was a large man with a boyish face, and he had often collaborated with Cheryl when she was at Kids&Company to get new products from prototype to full run. He'd seemed unflappable then— he'd always found a way to get the toys made quickly, without sacrificing the quality that gave Lakeland's products their specialness.

Cheryl dropped the report onto his desk. "This is just not going to cut it, Mark. Bull's-Eye Stores is looking for an exclusive line of wooden toys, and they'd love it to come from us. I know everyone thinks I'm crazy, but we *can* meet their pricing requirements—if we can establish manufacturing capabilities offshore in plenty of time to ship for Holiday."

"I know that, but . . ." Mark began.

"C'mon, Mark. You've been in this organization for more than 25 years. Running manufacturing for, what, 12?"

"Fourteen," he corrected her.

"Fourteen. So you know better than anyone that off-shore manufacturing is the future of this business. If we really want to grow Lakeland, we've got to go beyond the upscale market and get into the midmarket. We can't do that with our plants here; our costs are too high. But your report"—she tapped its cover with her forefinger—"says we should delay any move offshore for at least a year. You know as well as I do that that means losing the Bull's-Eye deal."

"I understand where you want to go, Cheryl. But we can't just hop on a plane to China and open a factory tomorrow. We'd be out of our league. What's more, it would take our focus off the manufacturing operation here."

"We don't have to build a factory, Mark. You know we can source this production. That's the only way we're going to get the Bull's-Eye contract—and as far as I can see, that contract is the only way we're going to meet the board's growth targets." Cheryl paced in front of his desk. "Did you call Cecil at Kids&Company, as I asked you to? He's sourcing private-label products from China, Indonesia, and the Philippines."

"We're playing telephone tag," Mark murmured. "But my bigger concern, Cheryl, is the union. Our contract is up in nine months, and you really don't want to go into negotiations at the same time you're moving manufacturing offshore."

"We're not talking about cutting jobs here in Minnesota. Hell, we're adding capacity."

"You know that I worked my way up from the floor, so I understand the union point of view. Believe me, they won't see this the way you do. They'll think it's the first step to outsourcing all our manufacturing. Frankly, I can't say I'd blame them."

"I don't think you understand. To meet our targets, we need to get Bull's-Eye on board. If we lose this contract, it's not going to be for lack of effort. Keep working on this—and be ready to talk about it at our meeting tomorrow." Then she added, "Mark, we go way

---

"Everyone here is in the slow lane. They're all wedded to the ways things have always been done."

---

back. I have full confidence in you. We can do this." She left him with an encouraging smile.

As Cheryl pulled out of the parking lot, she replayed a conversation she'd had earlier that day. Pat Sampsen, the head of Sampsen Design in Chicago, had called to say that he had picked up two packaging design awards—both for Kids&Company private-label products that she had spearheaded. She had been puzzled, though, when he told her that, no, he hadn't heard from Barry Quince, Lakeland's design director. She had pointedly asked Barry to give Pat a call two weeks ago. She was convinced that the local design firm Barry used just wasn't capable of top-notch work, and she wanted him to consider larger outfits like Sampsen Design.

"Why," she wondered, "does everyone up here seem to be dragging their feet? My manufacturing head doesn't want to manufacture overseas," she mused, "and my design director protects his little, mediocre design firm. I've been trying since my first week to get the procurement people to look at consolidating vendors for core parts, but you'd think I'd asked them to cut off their hands. Everyone here is in the slow lane. They're all wedded to the ways things have always been done.

"Maybe," she thought, "I need to bring in some fresh blood. If I could get Pat's firm for our packaging and marketing materials, and I could recruit Cecil from Kids&Company to work on outsourcing, I could start to tackle some of the other issues." She was feeling slightly more optimistic as she turned into her driveway.

Charting a Course

At 10:30 the next day, Cheryl and the management team gathered in the conference room. This space had been the CEO's office for generations, but when Cheryl came on board, she chose an office in the center of the executive floor and had this corner office converted into a conference room. She thought it was a good symbolic act: Things were going to be different, and she intended to be right in the thick of the action.

Mark was sitting at the round table, along with Elaine Spenser from marketing; Jerry Silistro from sales; and Ned Honester, the CFO.

"Let's get right to it," Cheryl began. "I've given you an overview of my vision for launching us into the midmarket, and this Bull's-Eye contract is a great place to start. As leaders in this company, you each play a key role. I'd like to hear your thoughts about how we move forward. Elaine, why don't you get us started?"

Elaine reported what Cheryl already knew: Research confirmed that the middle of the nonelectronic toy market was the only segment projected for double-digit growth, and those consumers were shopping at big chains like Bull's-Eye, not at specialty stores.

"So," she concluded, "I think we can launch a lower-priced line, provided it's differentiated, for the midmarket without cannibalizing our existing base."

"Great, Elaine." Cheryl had asked her to speak first because of Elaine's enthusiasm for undertaking new projects. Cheryl also realized that building momentum would be crucial in order to reach a consensus around her vision for the company.

"One more thing, Cheryl," Elaine said.

"Yes?"

"I don't want to overlook the branding issues. Every package we ship—and every delivery truck—is emblazoned with 'Handcrafted with pride in the USA.' We'll have to be extremely careful with the message we send, and we'll need to invest in more advertising. We don't want to face a backlash if people think we're not an American company any longer."

"Do you think you can handle it with the right resources?"

"It shouldn't be a problem. I'll light a fire under our ad firm, and I'll get Barry to work up new packaging ideas."

"Good. This could be a great chance for Barry to try working with Sampsen Design. Ask him to give them a call."

"Barry was thinking it would be fun for our local designers."

"I think it would be fun to have some world-class packaging," Cheryl said, nodding slowly at Elaine. "Have him call Sampsen. Now, Jerry, what do you see from a sales perspective?"

"Wait a second," Mark interrupted. He didn't want to drop the made-in-the-USA issue so quickly. He reminded Cheryl that when she was at Kids&Company, she had told him that Lakeland's U.S. manufacturing base was a great strength. He wanted to know what had changed and how she thought customers like Kids&Company would react to the move. Cheryl reminded him that when she'd made that comment, her priority was to maintain Kids&Company's competitive advantage. But now she needed to act in Lakeland's best interest, and that meant expanding into every viable market. As long as Lakeland was manufacturing only in the United States, its costs would be too high for it to sell in lower-priced markets. That said, she again asked Jerry to weigh in on sales.

Jerry also did exactly what Cheryl had come to expect. He expressed enthusiasm for the opportunity but then launched into a litany of reasons why he'd need significant new resources to handle it.

Cheryl was thinking about how best to respond when Mark said, "Jerry, let's talk about delivery. What do you think?"

"It's critical, of course—especially for Holiday. One of our biggest advantages is that we virtually always ship on time. Tresio has to ship across the Atlantic and get through customs—so there are many more opportunities for things to go wrong."

"I'm just wondering, Jerry, because our contract with the union is up fairly soon," said Mark. "What if this move leads to a slowdown or a strike? Where would that put us?"

Looking at Cheryl, Jerry replied, "It would be a disaster." He turned back to Mark and asked, "Do you think that would happen?"

Cheryl could feel the meeting swinging away from her, so she quickly asked Ned to weigh in.

"I want to remind everyone that the board has given us a very aggressive growth target. We can't forget that Mr. Swensen sold 30% of his holdings to Hastings,

Curtiss when he retired, and venture firms are relentless in their pursuit of growth. I know that Cheryl's plan may strike some of you as bold, but remember the first time she walked in here as a customer? We all thought she was nuts. She asked us to do some things that seemed crazy, but today those crazy ideas are some of our best-selling products. I'm looking at the bottom line, and I think that—while we have to be mindful of the issues raised here, of course—we need to move forward."

"I know that we have differing opinions," Cheryl said to the group. "But I also want you to know that I understand that we can only make this work as a team. Ned and I will present all of this to the board, and I expect everyone to get behind whatever decision is ultimately made."

She made a mental note to call Sean Curtiss to update him on the situation. His company held two of the seven seats on the board. The Swensen children had two. Wally Swensen made five. Karen Winks of Northern Minnesota Trust was the sixth, and Wally's old college roommate rounded out the numbers.

Rough Seas Ahead?

The next day, Cheryl was poring over her upcoming board presentation when she felt someone's eyes focusing on her.

"Wally," she said with surprise. "Look at how tan you are."

Swensen walked in and sat down. "I have to say that I like being CEO emeritus. I get to fish most of the time and just show up for the quarterly board meetings."

"It suits you," she smiled. His leathery face was a deep brown, and his white hair gave him a dashing air. She had been fond of Swensen from their first meeting. She'd been a young, hard-driven junior executive full of ideas, and he was a quiet, steady man who ran a long-standing company by making prudent decisions, sticking to its core value of quality, and eschewing fads. They had learned a lot from each other, and soon bold new products that were still true to Lakeland's heritage were flying off the Kids&Company store shelves.

"Lunch plans?" he asked. "I'd like to chat with you about the board presentation next week."

They both settled into a booth at Christie's—a mom-and-pop sandwich shop a few blocks from the office. They chose a booth toward the back where they could talk without being overheard. Two glasses of lemonade arrived without their needing to ask.

"What's on your mind, Wally?" Cheryl asked.

"I want you to think through what you're going to bring to the board," he said, gently. "Be sure you have all the implications mapped out."

"I'm just coming in with a more concrete plan for reaching the growth goals we set at the last meeting—that's all. There shouldn't be any big surprises."

"Really? I had dinner with Mark the other night, and he was telling me some of his reservations about the speed of your outsourcing plans. And I have to say,

I never thought I'd see our products in a store like Bull's-Eye."

"You had dinner with Mark?" Her voice was rising.

"He wasn't going behind your back, Cheryl. It was a family thing. He's my son's godfather, remember? We were just chatting."

"You knew I was going to change things when I came in. We talked about that. You wanted me to. And

---

"You have to understand, this is a very old company," said the former CEO. "You may need to pull people along more slowly to make sure you don't end up tearing the place apart."

---

when you sold a block of your shares to Hastings, Curtiss, you knew they were looking for growth. We're not going to do that by keeping things the way they are."

"You have to understand, this is a very old company," he said. "Some of the people who work for you, their parents and even grandparents worked here. What you're about to propose is going to scare them. Mark's not antiprogress by any means, but he does know this place better than anyone—except me. You may need to pull people along more slowly to make sure you don't end up tearing the place apart."

"If what we do works out, everyone here will be better off. I've already met with Cara and Wally V, and they support the move."

"I'm not certain that my children fully understand Mark's opposition."

It dawned on Cheryl right then that the board presentation might not go as well as she hoped. If Wally was cautioning her to slow down and Wally V turned out to be loyal to Mark, his godfather—well, it stood to reason that Cara would vote with the rest of the Swensen family.

"I don't want this to be a board showdown, Wally," said Cheryl, earnestly. "You hired me to grow this business. Let me do that."

"Whoa, slow down. There's not going to be any showdown. But you must see that you can't do this alone. You have to have your people's hearts and minds to make it a success."

"I have a plan." She told him about recruiting Cecil Flemming to take over new-product development. She went on to explain Cecil's expertise in overseas sourcing and her desire to have someone on the senior team who shared her style and speed.

Wally's brow furrowed slightly, signaling to Cheryl that this might be another move to ease into slowly, but he was finished arguing for the day. He sipped his lemonade, then replied diplomatically, "We're always eager to see great candidates. I'm sure he'd love working here."

"Wally, everyone who works here loves the place. I don't want to change that, but I do want to be sure that we all have a place to work five years out. I need you to have confidence in me now."

Is the CEO Pushing Too Much Change Too Quickly?

Four commentators offer expert advice.

➤ Kathleen Calcidise

Kathleen Calcidise is a vice president and the COO of Apple Retail Stores, headquartered in Cupertino, California.

Several years ago, I found myself in a turnaround situation with many parallels to Cheryl Hailstrom's. The company I signed on to lead had new external investors with high expectations about our growth potential and a management team resistant to the significant changes needed to hit those aggressive targets.

It's easy to see why Cheryl is frustrated. All the key indicators support her midmarket growth plan. She has a huge customer account in her sights and a legitimate sense of urgency; if Lakeland wants to ship in time for the holiday season, it has only a few months to design products, secure offshore production operations, and develop a marketing message that answers the branding issues. But she's saddled with a bunch of managers more interested in clinging to their familiar turf.

To get beyond this impasse, she'll have to make some changes. There's no reason she can't bring in experienced outsiders like Cecil and Pat, but she should pair them with members of the existing organization. I'd suggest appointing a team to guide the midmarket private-label development strategy and empowering the group with authority to do whatever is necessary to ensure on-time product delivery for the holidays.

Cheryl may also need to change her leadership style. What she sees as leading "by example" and relocating her office "to be right in the thick of the action" may be seen by others as coercion and intimidation. An emphasis on persuasion, inspiration, and negotiation might work better. She must start signaling her openness to hearing the concerns of people with divergent points of view.

Meanwhile, she needs to be communicating, consistently and enthusiastically, with her internal and external constituencies about how her growth strategy serves *all* their interests. Resistance to change will continue unless Cheryl can link her vision of expansion with their individual needs and expectations. I found, in my attempts to get some of the foot-dragging employees and board members to buy in to a vision, that it was best to frame it in bold contrasts. I compared the tangible future benefits of change for our organization, its employees, and its stakeholders with the dangers of doing nothing—which in our case would have involved bankruptcy and job losses. Whether Cheryl's message is as dramatic as that or not, it should aim to ensure that no one is blindsided by change. Surprises can only increase the fear and resistance that cause delays.

Perhaps most important, Cheryl needs to articulate a clear operating direction for Lakeland, one that specifies how structural and behavioral changes can be consistent with the company's most treasured values and norms *and* also improve performance. She can lead Lakeland's employees over barriers to change by affirming what they love about the place, even while she challenges comfortable ways of doing things.

To bring about cultural and performance transformation, I made it the explicit work of several teams. I charged them with identifying any obstacles to change and with recommending new structures, initiatives, and reward systems. By involving lots of employees, I was able to speed the process along.

I should stress that the company I worked for was in far more trouble than Lakeland. In two years, it went through three other CEOs, each with a different vision. When I came on board, time and money were running out, and internal expectations for my success were low indeed. Ultimately, several years after I moved on, the company did fail.

Cheryl, however, has a few advantages. Thanks to her past role with Lakeland, people there already believe in her.

That's a big leg up. Still, she may be mistaking how much license it gives her. Obviously, she hasn't felt she needed to spend much time building consensus for her potentially risky product-expansion plan. She thinks she's already earned the support of her colleagues and investors. I would caution her: She needs to earn it anew each day.

➤ Debra Benton

Debra Benton is the president of Benton Management Resources in Fort Collins, Colorado, and the author of Secrets of a CEO Coach *(McGraw-Hill, 1999).*

If Cheryl were my client, I'd point out that her relationship with the company has changed. She's no longer the customer, she's the boss. But she hasn't established the rules of engagement of working together.

To do so, she should privately explain to each individual on her team how she works. She might say something like, "I operate with full disclosure and mutual respect. I will never make you guess what I want, and I don't want to guess what you want. We must communicate relentlessly about how we will achieve our goals. And after we've discussed an issue, we will come up with one voice, which will be spoken up, down, and sideways in this organization." As Cheryl speaks, she'll smile, maintain a pass-the-salt tone of voice, and touch the person's arm.

Once the ground rules for effectively working together have been laid, Cheryl needs to address the goal of taking the company to the next level. The growth targets were set by the board and aren't up for debate, so the sole issue is how to achieve them.

Cheryl should ask each team member, "What do you see as a priority? What stands in the way of accomplishing that goal? How can we change that?" The priorities named in these individual conversations should then be put to the group for discussion. Once the team determines one voice on each issue, it can assign responsibility, create a strategy, and set a time frame.

If Mark Dawson continues to oppose the plan in management meetings, Cheryl must ask him to step outside to talk. The conversation could begin like this: "You may or may not be right in your assessment. We don't know yet. But we have all agreed to this plan. Supporting the plan to my face and then shooting it down later does not show respect. I know your opinion on the obstacles ahead. And I know you have a lot of experience here, but even the minimum-wage people can tell me why it *won't* work. You are the cream of the Lakeland crop, and your job is to make things happen that others thought couldn't be done.

"When I ran Kids&Company, you worked miracles—you found ways to get things made quickly without sacrificing quality. You need to perform that same magic now.

"When you have problems with what I say, please talk with me first; I will do the same with you. I don't want to be told about roadblocks for the first time in front of others. I work with a full-disclosure approach, and I expect the same of you. If you won't or can't, I'll hire someone who will." While she's talking, she should again be speaking calmly, have a relaxed smile, and stand where she can put her hand on his shoulder and grip just a little too tightly.

If Cheryl isn't clear with this team, she'll be no better with the next. She should not make personnel changes until she has given the current team a chance. Once she sees people's reactions, she can decide who stays, who goes, or who gets added.

In addition, Cheryl must have the rules-of-engagement discussion with Wally Swensen, members of the board, and the venture capitalists. No one must have any doubts about how she will lead. When Wally mentioned his discussion with Mark, Cheryl should have said (with, of course, a re-laxed smile, a pass-the-salt tone, and a firm touch), "You have always made prudent decisions in your business; that's why you hired me. We can take this company to the next level without sacrificing quality. I will provide you and the board, as I have the management team, with full disclo-sure about what we need to do and how we plan to do it. If someone or something is a sacred cow and cannot be touched, tell me now. And if that restriction compromises our objectives, I will readjust our profit estimates. But if you want me to effect change, some blood will be spilled."

If the chairman, the board, or the venture capitalists do not let Cheryl do the job she was hired to do, she must decide whether to stay or go. No job is permanent anyway.

➤ Dan S. Cohen

Dan S. Cohen is a partner at Deloitte Consulting (soon to be Braxton) in Irving, Texas, and the coauthor, with John P. Kotter, of The Heart of Change *(Harvard Business School Press, 2002).*

Cheryl has walked into Lakeland Wonders like a bull in a china shop. She wants to change the culture—she complains that they're all dragging their feet—but she's the one who's out of step. She has shown little respect for the operating style of this 94-year-old company. She hasn't been listening to senior managers, and she hasn't been talking to the board of directors to line up votes for the upcoming board meeting. She just expects everyone to follow her lead.

This is a very common mistake. Executives come in and say, "Here's my vision, let's go forward." But they fail to create any sense of urgency about why a change is required. In other words, they don't lay the groundwork to allow the change to take root. Unless Cheryl can figure out a way to get people excited about this new direction for the company, her vision will die a quick death. Mark is already throwing up roadblocks; he's concerned about the union's reaction to offshore manufacturing, and he's gone so far as to speak with the previous CEO. The head of marketing raises branding issues and resists working with a new design firm. And the sales director seems swayed by Mark's argument against offshore manufacturing. The only team member who supports Cheryl's plan is the CFO, and he's looking at it strictly from a numbers perspective.

For the team to come together, Cheryl has to stop talking about "my" vision and start acting on "our" vision. It appears that she and the senior management team never really developed a common vision of the company's future. If objectives aren't obvious to members of the top management team, what are the odds that the rest of the company will understand them, let alone get behind them?

My immediate advice for Cheryl is to take a minute to reflect on her performance over these past few months. In her quest to grow the company, she has done several things right: She moved out of the secluded corner office. She enhanced the bonus plan. She has tried to improve productivity. But the fact is, Cheryl hasn't thought through her strategy very well. For instance, union negotiations come up in nine months, but she hasn't yet brought a union rep into these discussions. She seems to think that the company will deal with the negotiations when the time comes. The same is true for the branding issue. Elaine says she can handle it, but she hasn't proposed a solid plan.

The most troubling aspect of Cheryl's performance is that her driving style isn't aligned with Lakeland's culture. She hasn't recognized that rather than increasing urgency, she is creating fear and anger among her executive group. If she doesn't adjust her operating style, she will continue to lose the confidence of key stakeholders. It's almost to the point that Wally, once her champion, fears that she could tear the company apart. And without Wally, she has no chance of winning the board's approval.

To regain Wally's trust, Cheryl must mend her relationship with Mark and show him why he should change his feelings and behavior to support her vision. If they put their heads together, Cheryl and Mark may come up with a new plan that addresses the growth goals and better fits Lakeland's culture. For instance, Lakeland might consider opening a subsidiary that does offshore production and sells to lower-end markets, thus eliminating some brand issues.

It's true that the board set aggressive growth goals, and Cheryl is working hard to meet them. But she can't do it alone. Unfortunately, she has yet to reach the emotions of the senior team, and she must if she's to ignite their active support of her change plan. Without that support, it doesn't matter if her vision is objectively sound; it won't get off the ground until she deals effectively with the current level of complacency among her senior team.

➤ Nina Aversano

Nina Aversano has held executive positions at IBM, Xerox, AT&T, and Lucent Technologies, among other companies. Currently, she runs her own consulting practice in Kinnelon, New Jersey.

It seems that Cheryl believes that her plan is the only way to grow the business. I fell into that trap when I was starting my career at IBM. I knew my proposals were right, so I was frustrated that I had to spend time convincing others that my ideas needed to be implemented without delay. Then a wise and seasoned manager said to me, "Nina, people support what they create. You need to engage others in the creation process, or you are doomed to failure." What a lesson! I had believed that involving more people in the planning process would slow things down, but in fact, the opposite is true.

Cheryl also needs to learn a related lesson: "There's more than one way to rope a calf." A Xerox veteran with a pronounced Texas drawl told me that. I'd been hired to launch a line of word processors, and I can remember looking at my colleagues as though they were the "great unwashed." They'd never sold in this nontraditional (that is, non-copier related) market; they didn't understand the technology; and, in my mind, they had no understanding of how to build a launch plan to meet our aggressive objectives. But this experienced manager wouldn't let me discount the thinking of others. He patiently discussed the alternative views and forced me to see that there are many ways to succeed. It wasn't easy, but I learned to try other people's solutions—and I found that approach very liberating. Cheryl might, too. It seems crazy that she hasn't asked Mark, her key manufacturing manager, for his solution, especially since he's delivered for her in the past.

Like Cheryl, I've also had to deal with unions. I joined AT&T Network Systems (the offspring of Western Electric—a 100-year-old manufacturing, R&D, and distribution arm of the former Bell System)—in 1990. Bill Marx, the president, chose leaders who he thought could change the culture of this former monopoly without wreaking havoc. I headed up an organization of roughly 1,500 installers and managers; most were members of the powerful Communications Workers of America and the International Brotherhood of Electrical Workers. They were predominantly white men, aged 48 or older, with high school educations. They were well trained, dedicated, and highly respected by the customers. But the unit was hemorrhaging money.

When I walked in the door, I felt as if I had been thrown into some alien culture; I wasn't sure how to begin to turn things around. I knew I needed the knowledge that these managers possessed, but it was clear they didn't want me there. So I began by reviewing the financials. Then I met with every local union president to go over the state of the business in detail—the good, the bad, and the ugly. And you know what? With the exception of one old, crusty union chief, I got a great reception (and even he came around eventually). Then I held town meetings with all the employees, in groups of 50 or fewer. It was usually just the rank and file and me—I didn't want lots of supervisors there to constrain the questions.

It was one of the most valuable learning experiences of my career. Those people were the heart and soul of the business. They wanted it to succeed, and they were open-minded enough to let me share the realities of the business and seek their opinions and ideas. Together, we turned our losses around and built a highly competitive machine. Cheryl would be well served to talk to the union members about her plans and solicit their help in making Lakeland more competitive.

Finally, our young CEO needs to recalibrate the board's expectations. Yes, growth is needed, but the targets must be realistic. The "growth at any cost" mind-set will be disastrous for this company. Cheryl has many of the right ingredients to make a great leader. She needs to move with speed and intensity to build a new culture from the strong foundation she has been given.

Originally published in October 2002

Reprint R0210A

DIANE L. COUTU

Too Old to Learn?

Executive Summary

C.J. Albert, the head of family-owned Armor Coat Insurance, is just settling in on a Sunday evening when he receives an unsettling phone call from his star salesman. Fifty-two-year-old Ed McGlynn has just returned from a business dinner with his younger technology mentor, and he's none too happy with the way he's being treated. If C.J. doesn't take this attack dog off him, Ed warns, he's gone.

C.J. had indeed assigned 28-year-old Roger Sterling—the company's monomaniacal, slightly antisocial director of e-commerce—to teach Ed about digital strategy and the Web. Reverse mentoring seemed like a good way to create a digital insurance product that would allow Armor Coat to keep up with its competitors.

But there'd been tension between Ed and Roger right from the start—stemming from their personalities and their two departments. So when the two reluctantly agreed to meet for dinner to talk, the conversation didn't go well. Ed insisted that great sales reps, not the Internet, are crucial to selling insurance. Roger insisted that the Web will revolutionize the way insurance is sold and distributed—that Ed either give in or move on. Ed took off in a huff and subsequently phoned C.J. Roger followed Ed's irate call with his own weary ultimatum: "Either Ed goes or I go."

C.J. faces some difficult Monday morning discussions with both disgruntled parties. What should he do? Six commentators, including a mentor-protégé pair, offer their advice in this fictional case study.

C.J. loved *Law and Order*. He seldom had time to watch TV anymore, but when he did, he wanted something unsentimental. As a rerun of the show came on, he settled into the taupe leather sofa in the living room and adjusted his glasses. Just then, the phone rang.

Even now that he was CEO of Armor Coat Insurance, the Providence, Rhode Island-based property and casualty insurance company that he had inherited from his father, there was still one thing that C.J. could not do—let a phone go unanswered. Not even on a Sunday night. He sighed and picked up the receiver.

"C.J.? I've been looking everywhere for you." The voice at the other end of the line was angry and intense, and C.J. knew instantly that it belonged to Ed McGlynn, the company's star salesman.

Ed had been named top performer six of the last ten years and had pulled in most of Armor Coat's major accounts. Customers loved him. At 52, he was still the magnetic and popular hockey hero that he had been at Notre Dame. He took his major clients sailing on weekends and played golf with them during the week.

Whenever he recounted his triumphs, Ed would brag about how more than 300 of Armor Coat's customers had sent him get-well cards after he'd had his appendix out. Now, on the phone, Ed was clearly upset.

"I've been with this company 23 years, and I've given it everything I've got," he fumed. "But if you don't get rid of that SOB you sicced on me, I'm out of here. Those Internet guys don't speak the same language we do. They're arrogant. They lack respect. They don't have the same values. And I'll tell you, C.J., I'm not just some stupid salesman who's going to sit back while some baby-faced know-it-all squeezes the life out of me."

New Tricks of the Trade

The know-it-all was Roger Sterling, the 28-year-old Web guru that C.J. had hired last year to be the director of electronic commerce at Armor Coat—and the mentor that C.J. had assigned to work with Ed on his computer skills.

With his entrepreneurial flair, and a monomaniacal focus on business, Roger seemed typical of the breed of software engineers that flourished in Silicon Valley. He had studied math at Cal Tech for a year and was second in his class before he dropped out to join a $20 million start-up. Born with a sense of entitlement and a conviction that the rest of the world was irrelevant, Roger had a reputation for his technological savvy—

and for his nonexistent people skills. After the IPO, he was not only richer but also brasher than before.

Roger took the job at Armor Coat only because he was convinced that the insurance industry was ripe for an e-commerce revolution. Insurance was, after all, a product that consisted purely of information and money. Already, he understood the possibilities of the Internet the way few people in the insurance industry did. For him, it was simply a game to push the technology to its limits—without regard for the people who would use it. When C.J. approached him about restructuring a national program to sell insurance directly to customers on the Web, Roger knew exactly what the potential was: "We can eliminate about 2,000 agents. It's a license to print money."

The odd thing was, Roger had a hard time understanding why some people might object to a cavalier attitude like his. C.J. chalked it up to generational differences. If Roger had emotions, he hid them well—so well that the senior salespeople called him "Pac Man." His robotic reputation was only reinforced by the fact that he didn't seem to have any outside interests. He didn't play sports, he didn't fish—he didn't seem to do anything but drive to and from work in his BMW convertible.

"Yes, if I could invite only one of the men to my club, it would definitely be Ed," C.J. said to himself. And now Ed's ego clearly needed massaging. C.J. sympathized with his star salesman—he himself knew little about computers. But at the same time, he realized there was no going back to the predigital age. Armor Coat had to move into the Web era or it would die.

Legacy of Change

Indeed, change had been the norm at the French-Canadian company that the Albert family had founded as a four-man operation in 1879. Since then, Armor Coat was where all the Albert men had cut their teeth. A few old hands still remembered C.J.'s legendary grandfather Anatole, who had run the company with an iron fist. But it was C.J.'s father who had done the most to make the company what it was today: a nationally recognized corporation with offices in 32 states. By the time C.J. took the helm in the late 1980s, Armor Coat's sales and profits were skyrocketing. The company finally went public in 1996.

The IPO had made the Albert family extremely rich—C.J. himself was a millionaire many times over. Still in the afterglow, C.J. knew that the family and other shareholders trusted him to keep things on track. That meant staying devoted to the customer and keeping costs down. The latter was especially challenging given that many traditional insurance firms were considering going on-line. Internet-only start-ups had already discovered cheaper, more efficient ways to replace the ingrained and expensive agent networks, and C.J. knew that Armor Coat could ignore this option only at its peril.

Yet no company to date had found a way to over-come the customer's desire for human contact. It was understandable that people might not want to buy in-surance—a product often associated with death and

---

Armor Coat needed to draw on Ed's strength in customer relations and on Roger's strength in cutting-edge technology.

---

disaster—through an impersonal intermediary such as a computer. The challenge, as C.J. saw it, was to find a way to make the digital product friendly and unintimi-dating. To do that, he reckoned, Armor Coat needed to draw on both Ed's strengths (solid customer relation-ships) and Roger's (cutting-edge technology). The older generation and the new needed to come together to make this work.

That wasn't going to be easy. There'd been tension between the company's salespeople and Roger's de-partment right from the start. Internet experts didn't come cheap. In fact, C.J. had to offer them salaries that were equal to the money being paid to sales agents who had already been in the field for 15 or 20 years. It was inevitable that those agents would resent the "over-paid" newcomers. C.J. also decided that the new Web designers would report directly to Roger. C.J. realized that Roger's management position could stir angry feelings among the salespeople and concerns about company priorities. But he knew the new technology recruits would need lots of support and responsibility if the transformation was really going to work. All that was bad enough, but then C.J. fired 10% of the sales force to cut costs. The reaction was severe: the survivors felt betrayed. The salespeople blamed the Web designers for the organizational grenade that had been tossed into their midst.

Who's in Charge?

C.J. had hung up the phone and was sitting on the sofa, deep in thought. His wife Karen walked into the living room, noticed that the TV was on mute, and read her husband's expression. "What's wrong?" she asked. Karen was a child psychologist and the mother of their two children, Annie and Simon. C.J. and Karen had been married almost 25 years, and she knew everything there was to know about him and the business.

"Things are coming unglued," C.J. sighed. "Ed just called, and he's hopping mad about some blowup he had with Roger Sterling. I'm beginning to give up hope that this mentoring thing is ever going to work between them."

C.J. picked up the remote control again and returned to the last moments of *Law and Order*. Just before the end, a commercial came on for on-line stock brokerage

Ameritrade. It featured a young office worker whose boss interrupts him from photocopying his face for party invitations—not to reprimand him but to ask for

---

"Like it or not, it's the younger generation that will have to mentor us rather than the other way around," C.J. mused. "And that's a big problem for guys like Ed."

---

his help buying stocks on-line. The young guy shows his boss how to navigate the Web—and then explodes into an exuberant dance and invites his boss to the party.

"Well, it certainly isn't working out that way at Armor Coat, is it," C.J. blurted, lifting himself off the sofa and walking across the room to the bookshelf. He picked up a volume of the *Encyclopaedia Britannica* and absentmindedly flipped though the pages. "Like it or not, it's the younger generation that will have to mentor us rather than the other way around," C.J. mused. "And that's a big problem for guys like Ed. He's so proud—and so suspicious of technology. And so reluctant to change. But change is the only thing kids know."

A New Kind of Mentor

C.J. had, in fact, tried to do exactly what the Ameritrade commercial had depicted. Armor Coat's HR department earlier in the year had initiated a reverse-mentoring program: all salespeople were strongly encouraged to choose a young mentor who could teach them how to store and call up information from Armor Coat's new on-line databases and how to surf the Web. The thought was, if the customer-focused salespeople understood the Web more, they could help Armor Coat use the Internet to boost profits and improve service.

When C.J. discovered that Ed had failed to pick a mentor, he decided to assign Roger to work with him. What Roger lacked in people skills, he made up for in sheer smarts and in his interest in insurance—two virtues that Ed admired a lot. C.J. even dared to hope that Ed would be flattered to get one-on-one attention from the company's tech guru.

"Give Ed space to ask you naive questions. He's got to learn about things he's not familiar with," C.J. counseled Roger. "But listen to his questions, too, because he knows a lot about our customers."

Roger was less than optimistic. He thought the whole experiment was a waste of time. "What's at stake is not a few computing skills but the fact that guys like Ed have to learn to think about the business in an entirely new way," he told C.J. "Ed needs a complete change in mind-set, and I can't manage that by teaching him a few tricks on the computer. In themselves, computer training classes are pointless."

The relationship didn't get better from there. Only last Monday, a furious Roger had called C.J. to complain that Ed had skipped a critical meeting outlining how the Web would create a more efficient interface between insurers and their customers. "That fast-talking jock isn't a team player," Roger protested vehemently.

C.J. didn't have time to deal with the call just then. The board meeting was coming up, and he was deep into preparing a presentation on the company's quarterly results—which for the first time in 12 years were dipping. "Can't you guys work out your differences?" he asked. "Just sit down and try to work through the problem." When Ed rang three minutes later to complain about the same meeting, C.J. blew up. "I don't want to hear about it anymore. My God, Ed, you're twice his age. Fix it!"

The Dinner That Didn't

Reluctantly, Roger and Ed agreed to meet at the Wild Ginger that Sunday night to try to patch things up. It was the first time they had ever sat down for a meal together, and Ed was late. He'd been shuttling his kids back and forth to soccer games all day, and he was tired.

When he got to the restaurant, Roger was already seated at a table, sipping green tea. "Ah, you're drinking my daughter's favorite," Ed said, trying to make small talk. "She's quite the computer one, she is." Roger smiled politely but said nothing. Ed found his irritation mounting at the company for putting someone as socially inept as Roger Sterling in a position of authority.

He ordered a double shot of Jameson's, and then unfolded his chopsticks and started delicately poking around at the eel and California maki that Roger had ordered as an appetizer. Ed was the first to broach the subject. "C.J. said we should get together and try to iron out some of our differences," he said, weighing every word. "Maybe for the sake of Armor Coat, we can make some of these innovations work."

Roger's response was quick and nonchalant. "They are working," he said. "I told C.J. that. We're right on course. My team is getting things done even faster than scheduled."

Roger's retort made Ed clench his fists under the table. "I'm not stupid, Roger," his voice shook. "I may be many things, but I'm not stupid. The Web is changing distribution, yes, but great sales reps are and always will be the key to the insurance business. People don't buy insurance—you sell it to them. They don't think about their mortality—you gently remind them of it. I know how this business works. I've been doing it since before you were out of diapers."

Roger had heard this story before, and his eyes moved up when waiters passed by the table. Ed was deeply annoyed by Roger's reaction but pressed on. "Let's put our cards on the table," he said finally. "I don't like the way you and the other 'whiz kids' have been treating us in sales. You're condescending. You routinely schedule meetings on short notice without even checking whether it's a good time for us. You don't respect our experience."

Roger leaned in toward Ed. "Look," he said, trying to be conciliatory, "I'm not saying work in the field doesn't pay off. But I don't think you realize how much the customer's mentality is changing. People want information fast. They want to be able to compare the numbers and the services, and that's a lot easier to do on-line. As I see it, you have two options: you can join the team, or you can leave the team. It sounds brutal, but the younger people in sales are *getting* it."

Ed was horrified. "Let me give you some advice, kid," he said, reaching for his wallet. "Don't ever go into PR." Ed slammed enough cash on the table to cover dinner for both of them. He pulled his coat close to his chest, turned on his heel, and stormed out of the restaurant. "You're a million miles away," said Karen, turning off the TV while C.J. was still flipping through the encyclopedia.

"I was just thinking that mentoring seemed so much easier in my day when it was clear who did what," her husband explained. "Wisdom got passed down through the generations. But these days it's people who've dropped out of school who have the edge."

"I don't think it's all that strange," Karen countered. "We learn from our kids, don't we? And I always learn from my patients."

"Yeah, but when we were kids, Karen, I was an expert on stamps. You were an expert on Nancy Drew.

Today's kids are experts on a global revolution that is affecting every aspect of our lives. No wonder Ed feels like he's losing control."

Just then, the phone rang again. This time it was Roger. He sounded tired—and fed up. "C.J., I'm a digital expert, not an expert on fixing the egos of insecure, middle-aged salesmen. That's just not what I came to Armor Coat for. Either McGlynn leaves the team, or I do. That's your decision. I'll be around tomorrow if you want to talk."

C.J. replaced the phone in its cradle and relayed the latest news to Karen. "What am I going to do?" he asked with deep frustration in his voice. "I don't need a generation gap at Armor Coat. I need these guys to connect. Otherwise, we won't be here in five years."

What Should C.J. Do?

Six commentators offer their advice.

➤ Monica C. Higgins

Monica C. Higgins is an assistant professor of organizational behavior at Harvard Business School in Boston.

The events at Armor Coat do not describe mentoring, reverse or otherwise. We have a situation in which a young new-hire has been charged with teaching a salesman who has been with the company 23 years how to surf the Web. If it works, such a program might constitute coaching of some sort, but it is certainly not true mentoring, which involves both career and psychosocial support, such as friendship and caring.

At bottom, this case is about organizational change—about a successful, family-run insurance business that needs to change the way it delivers services to customers. To effectively move Armor Coat in a new direction, C.J. Albert should be leading the charge. Instead, the CEO delegates the organizational change effort to Roger Sterling—a newcomer who does not seem to care about anything except money and technology. This is both unrealistic and bound to fail.

It's no surprise that at the end of the case, we have two valuable employees, Roger and Ed McGlynn, who are both ready to leave the company in a huff. The attempt to institute a reverse-mentoring program has clearly failed. Let's see why. From the case, we know that C.J. has appointed Roger to mentor Ed. Yet research suggests that a mentoring relationship works best when it evolves over time, in an informal fashion, through a shared interest in professional development. This was clearly not the case at Armor Coat.

Other research shows that effective mentoring relationships are those in which the communication styles of the mentor and protégé match one another. Here, the opposite is true. Ed enjoys interacting one-on-one with people, developing such strong relationships with his clients that they send him get-well cards. Roger has a robotic style. Clearly, this was not the right match—much less the right conditions under which C.J. could have ever expected a true mentoring relationship to flourish.

Beyond his poor understanding of mentoring relationships, C.J. seems oblivious to the emotional fallout from the change effort at Armor Coat. His own diagnosis? "Generational differences," he says, and at one point he even orders Ed to "Fix it!" This diagnosis does not address the real problem: as Ed clearly tells Roger at their ill-fated dinner meeting, the senior sales staff feels that its experience is not respected.

Ed's feelings are certainly not the bailiwick of *any* generation, be they 20-somethings or 40-somethings. Yet his complaint underscores a fundamental problem in this case: no change program can succeed simply by imposing a mechanistic mentoring program from above on employees who are struggling with a widespread transformation effort and who lack genuine respect for one another.

Perhaps it is C.J.'s wife Karen who understands best what's at stake. She recognizes that Armor Coat will have to integrate the young people if it is going to change. But she doesn't see anything fundamentally new about that. She always learns from her younger patients, she says. So, too, in today's information-based economy, knowledge may be king, but it's the sharing that takes place between young and old that is essential.

C.J. will need both Roger and Ed to change Armor Coat. But before any sort of meaningful change effort—or even mentoring—can get under way, C.J. needs to exercise real leadership. He already understands that both Roger and Ed have their strengths, but he has failed to communicate that. He can begin there—it's not too late. After all, both men have turned to him for advice and counsel. Now it's C.J.'s turn to mentor.

➤ Lloyd Trotter

Lloyd Trotter is the CEO and president of GE Industrial Systems in Plainville, Connecticut.

There's an obvious lack of fit between Roger Sterling and Ed McGlynn in the reverse-mentoring program at Armor Coat, and C.J. should take immediate steps to end that relationship. But the trouble at Armor Coat goes deeper than a personality clash between these two men.

Roger is not just a poor mentor, he is also an employee who is out of sync with the company's core values. His attitude does not mesh with the values of teamwork and camaraderie that have long driven corporate culture at Armor Coat. So apart from the mentoring question, C.J. has to decide whether or not to keep Roger.

Just as important, C.J. has to find some way to undo the damage to Ed. His top salesperson's ego and self-esteem have been badly bruised. Given the current business pressures, C.J. can't afford to have Ed become disengaged. Alienating him could have devastating effects on his productivity and, ultimately, on the company's bottom line. Ed's situation must be addressed as soon as possible.

But Ed should get more than fuzzy words of reassurance from C.J. He deserves assistance in his efforts to accommodate all the changes that are currently unfolding at Armor Coat. At GE, we've learned that if an executive closes himself off from learning new things, he is putting his career in jeopardy—and the company's success at risk. Ideally, there should be an intervention from human resources.

After resolving these issues, C.J. has to reposition reverse mentoring more positively to his employees. To a large extent, it seems as though the program was created from the top down and forced on warring camps in the company. The business has a rich family history and a strong work ethic, so it seems as though Armor Coat's employees would more likely accept reverse mentoring if it were positioned as a tool for collaboration rather than as an us-versus-them blockade.

Armor Coat also needs to reexamine how it matches individuals. The company must take into account the dynamics of the people involved in the reverse mentoring relationship. C.J. needs to seek out best practices from other companies. How do they screen mentoring candidates? What personality traits make the best matches? What should the expectations be on both sides of the relationship?

Lastly, the idea of reverse mentoring needs to be introduced prudently. I know that when I was presented with the possibility of having a younger person mentor me, I found it a bit daunting at first. But for both of us, the reverse-mentoring program at GE has been an excellent tool for mutual learning and growth. I believe that the key to our success is that no matter at what level we find ourselves in the organization, we can accept change. Those who cannot become obsolete in our organization.

Meeting with my mentor has made us both more ready for change, and we quickly recognized numerous learning and teaching opportunities that cut both ways.

I've learned a lot about the Internet from my mentor, and I've been able to experience and see firsthand the bright, young talent that represents the future leadership of my business. At the same time, my mentor has had a tremendous opportunity to learn what it's like to be a CEO. If we had both closed ourselves off from these experiences, it would have been a senseless waste. That's how I see it for anyone who is not open to learning—top down or bottom up. It's slamming down the gate on your own future.

It's not too late for C.J. to make reverse mentoring work at Armor Coat. By learning from this experience, he can begin to develop some best practices that will not only help his company become an e-business but also raise the bar for other companies that want to launch a reverse-mentoring program.

➤ Steven Luria Ablon

Steven Luria Ablon is an associate clinical professor of psychiatry at Harvard Medical School and at Massachusetts General Hospital, both in Boston. He is also a training and supervising adult and child analyst at the Boston Psychoanalytic Society and Institute.

My father, who was the CEO of a *Fortune* 500 company, often told me that progress occurs when old men die and young men take over. I argued the point with him. My view is that real progress occurs when people are open to learning from mentors, regardless of their age. And an essential characteristic of good mentoring is openness, by both parties, to the complexities of the other person's experience.

At Armor Coat, neither Ed nor Roger has any real interest in trying to understand the other's experience. We don't know exactly why, but it may have to do with their own vulnerable self-esteem or how they identify with authority figures, such as parents or siblings.

Whatever the reasons for the antagonism between Ed and Roger, it's up to C.J. to find a creative way to help his employees work together. By sending the two men out to dinner alone, C.J. abdicated his responsibility. Rather than assume that he understands their experience, he should sit down with them and immerse himself in their viewpoints.

C.J. needs to establish an environment in which Ed and Roger feel comfortable sharing their experiences and concerns. By fostering such an exchange, C.J. would be mentoring his two subordinates by letting them see the importance of openness and co-mentoring. He could then use that experience to demonstrate to Ed and Roger how the two men can learn from each other—and turn Armor Coat into a company that makes the best use of the old and new economies.

Let me use a clinical experience to illustrate how this can work.

In my work as a child psychoanalyst, I always learn from my patients. One such patient was a ten-year-old named Harry. His parents brought him to me because over the course of a year, Harry had looked sad, was often tearful, and was constantly daydreaming in class. After Harry got to know me and began to feel comfortable in the office, he told me he wanted to play chess. He announced that he was very good at chess. We played the game several times, and it turned out that his way of playing the game was quite unusual. Whenever he faced a difficult situation, he would announce a new rule that gave his pieces unusual powers. Then he would defeat me soundly.

As the games continued, Harry told me that the queen was actually a very weak piece. He explained that the queen was weak because she had to spend so much time watching out for the king, who really could do very little for himself. Over time, Harry and I came to understand how the game related to his life. In the past year, his father had developed asthma and on several occasions had life-threatening attacks. Harry's mother lived in terror that her husband would die suddenly. She gave up her usual activities in order to be available in case of an emergency. In this context, family life became chaotic and confusing. Harry felt that his home life had become unpredictable and precarious.

Harry and I were mentors to each other. I learned from Harry that he didn't need help with the rules of chess or to be able to accept losing; he needed someone to understand the broader experience at the root of his behavior. At the same time, Harry began to realize that I was interested in exploring and understanding his conflicting and confusing feelings and experiences. He learned that I wanted to understand him, not judge him.

If they are to learn from each other, Ed and Roger need to try to be open in a similar way. They need to understand that by working together and embracing their differences they will ultimately be able to harness each other's strengths to help build a successful business. They both have unique contributions to offer. But to have any chance of working well together, they're going to need C.J. to step in and lead by example.

Learning about the complexity of another person's experience is essential in all relationships and crucial for a vital and satisfying life. Although I don't always agree with my dad, I've learned a lot from him over the years. Understanding our differences brings us even closer.

➤ Stuart Pearson and Mohan Mohan

Stuart Pearson is marketing services IT manager for Procter & Gamble in the United Kingdom and Ireland.

Mohan Mohan is vice president of the health and beauty care division of P&G in the United Kingdom and Ireland.

The real problem in the reverse-mentoring relationship between Ed and Roger is the huge amount of fear and insecurity in both players. C.J. may not be able to salvage them as a team, but he may be able to use the conflict to learn valuable lessons about the nature of mentoring and change.

The brash, steely-eyed but technologically brilliant Roger actually has a lot to teach Ed about competing successfully and profitably in the networked economy—despite what Roger thinks about computer training being "pointless." It isn't just by luck that Roger has positioned himself as a Web guru in an industry that is ripe for an on-line revolution. He is not afraid of change or hierarchy, and in our experience that's a good trait for young mentors to have. Reverse mentors can't be easily intimidated; they need the self-confidence to set challenges for their protégés or the relationship won't work.

Roger's role as mentor should be to stoke Ed's enthusiasm for technology—but C.J. also needs to convince Roger that he, in turn, has something to learn from Ed. Without this mutual deference, no mentoring relationship can ever work, reverse or otherwise.

This is where Roger's lack of people skills gets him in trouble. Not only is he unable to increase Ed's comfort level with technology, but Roger seems uncertain whether he even wants to reach out to Ed. At this point, C.J. must convince Roger to step back from his mission of pushing technology to its limits and take stock of the interpersonal factors at play. That would be a big first step toward improving the relationship.

Of course, Ed has his own issues that he has to come to terms with: there are the new-hire salaries, the layoffs in the sales department, and perhaps even fears about growing older. And although Ed is great at what he does—the numbers show that—he is unwilling to learn how to conduct business in a changing electronic world. All his antics, from bailing out of a training session with Roger to failing to pick a mentor in the first place, point to a man who is afraid to change his good-old-boy ways of selling insurance.

Ed may never become a technology expert, but he needs to take a more proactive approach to getting this new training and information. This is where HR could help, perhaps by creating a customized program to introduce Ed to the technological skills he so badly needs.

No matter what happens to Roger and Ed, C.J. shouldn't give up on the concept of reverse mentoring—it can be a powerful tool. But C.J. should realize that mentoring has a delicate bond at its core—one that can't be forced. P&G's reverse-mentoring program is voluntary, and it has worked beautifully time and again. Even though the working relationship between the two of us fit into an overall training initiative here at P&G, we originally came together because we wanted to, not because we were assigned to one another. We arrange mutually convenient times to meet. We don't consider the age gap a burden but an opportunity that enriches our business and personal relationships—whether we are talking about PalmPilots or work-life balance.

The reverse-mentoring program at P&G has another benefit—it spreads the knowledge base throughout the company, which is crucial to any organization's success. There are many ways to get conversations going in a company, but reverse mentoring is one of the best. And all it takes is a genuine willingness to learn.

Indeed, our own experiences with reverse mentoring at P&G have been deeply guided by Alvin Taylor's observation that "in the twenty-first century, an illiterate is not one who cannot read or write, but one who is unwilling to learn, unlearn, and relearn."

➤ Yoram "Jerry" Wind

Yoram "Jerry" Wind is the Lauder Professor of Marketing at University of Pennsylvania's Wharton School in Philadelphia. He has been leading the development of the Wharton e-Fellows program, which includes a reverse-mentoring component that matches senior executives with Wharton students.

This CEO must be extremely frustrated after getting off to such a promising start with his efforts to bring Armor Coat into the digital era by creating an "unintimidating" on-line insurance product. C.J. hired a highly qualified technology person, Roger, and empowered him to lead the company through its Internet revolution. He rightly recognized the need to integrate Roger's on-line expertise with Ed's understanding of customers' needs—and instituted a reverse-mentoring program to create that synergy.

But despite his best intentions, C.J. now has a couple of extremely unhappy players on his hands—high performers who represent the two functional groups that lie at the core of C.J. and Armor Coat's e-transformation strategy.

So what happened? As I see it, there are three fatal flaws in C.J.'s strategy. First off, the CEO planned to implement companywide change through the functional silo of technology rather than through a cross-functional team.

Next, he neglected the organizational architecture. He failed to alter the culture and the compensation systems so they could assist the e-transformation at Armor Coat.

Finally, C.J. didn't create an effective reverse-mentoring program.

Reverse mentoring, to work effectively, should be a non-threatening, supportive, and educational experience for both parties. So the selection of a mentor is as critical as the choice of a coach in any professional sport; it requires careful thought and consideration. For instance, you wouldn't have Andre Agassi coach Pete Sampras while the two still compete aggressively against each other. Assigning Roger to coach Ed is just as inappropriate.

From Ed's perspective, Roger is the enemy. His arrival prompted the layoffs of Ed's friends and colleagues, and his impersonal way of transacting business goes against everything that Ed believes in. From Roger's perspective, Ed is not a colleague in need but someone who stands in the way of progress.

Given the intense opposition of these men, the relationship forced by C.J. was bound to fail.

The mentor and protégé must share a common objective, and there must be trust between the two parties. The right mentor for Ed would be a young person with expertise in technology—and someone who can show empathy and interest in Ed's mastering the technology necessary to take Armor Coat into the next millennium. The mentor should also show a healthy respect for the skills that Ed brings to the table. Given his personality, maybe Roger should not mentor at all.

A final point: reverse mentoring can solidify collaboration among functional groups, but it cannot be the only tool that enforces such teamwork or the sole catalyst for change, as seems to be the expectation here. Rather, effective reverse mentoring is a by-product of good communication that already exists between functional groups. Even the best mentor-protégé relationships have their limits.

Originally published in November–December 1999

Reprint R00605

JULIA KIRBY

The Cost Center

That Paid Its Way

Executive Summary

Eric Palmer arrived at the top floor of Camden Robotics, a supplier of industrial automation tools, excited to tell CEO Tom O'Reilly about his latest win: a print ad account with a well-known local software maker. "You pulled in more business?" the boss responded. "It's really working out, then, isn't it?"

Six months earlier, Palmer, the head of marketing communications at Camden, had been in a less optimistic mood as he'd walked into the executive suite. His department had recently expanded and hired some pricey designers, but because of the economic slowdown, Camden was launching fewer marketing campaigns, and Palmer had feared that his department would be targeted for layoffs.

Executive Summary

Instead, O'Reilly proposed recasting the marketing function as a business unit. It would continue to provide services to other units within the company, but it would also be free to engage in "value pricing" and could propose project work internally just as outside agencies might. In addition, the new group, Creative Central, could serve customers outside of Camden in its spare time to earn revenue to defray its expenses.

At first, the reaction to the news was overwhelmingly positive across the company. Palmer was thriving in the role of corporate entrepreneur, updating O'Reilly frequently about the deals his unit was making. But several months into the change, the complaints started. Other internal units felt overcharged for marketing services, ignored by a busy Palmer and his people, and awkwardly left out of the loop in those cases where Palmer's outside clients intersected with Camden's mainstream clients.

As the discontent grows, O'Reilly is left to decide whether this organizational change is working. Four commentators weigh in on this fictional study.

"Well, Eric. You look like the cat that ate the canary. What's up?" Grace Tansky, the matronly assistant to CEO Tom O'Reilly, couldn't help but comment as she watched an obviously pleased with himself Eric Palmer bound up the steps toward her. This was the executive suite, the topmost of the floors occupied by Camden Robotics, and she was the gatekeeper.

"Another new client," Eric called out with a grin. "BlinkWare wants us to do some print ads. Now we just have to learn something about the software business." As he approached Grace's desk, he glanced toward O'Reilly's office door, slightly ajar. "Is he interruptible? Or should I just leave a voice mail?"

It was the boss who answered, though. "Hey, Eric. What's this I hear? You pulled in some business?" As he strode out into the hallway, Tom extended his hand to shake Eric's. "That's great to hear. It's really working out, then, isn't it? See, I told you so." Grace watched, half smiling, as the two walked together to the coffee station down the hall, with Eric giving Tom a play-by-play of the win.

A Cost Center Comes of Age

It was only six months ago that a more subdued Eric Palmer had been ushered into his boss's suite. The company had come to an abrupt awareness that it would have to cut costs. Camden supplied industrial automation tools to midsize and large manufacturing companies and had a sizable consulting business besides. But as the economy softened, a few of Camden's largest customers had experienced declining orders from their clients, and in short order, the slowdown had worked its way up the supply chain to Camden.

It was terrible timing for Eric, the ambitious and likable fellow who headed up Camden's marketing communications department. He had campaigned successfully to increase his staff and had recruited some truly creative—and high-priced—talent. At the same time, he'd won funds to do an extensive technology overhaul, which would enable his group to get serious about Web-based communications. All this was approved with the expectation that Camden's business units would launch more aggressive marketing campaigns and would require more support from Eric's headquarters-based group.

But in a downturn, that spending looked like unnecessary overhead. Business units were trimming their marketing plans, not beefing them up. And even Eric had to admit that, in the hunt for cost-cutting targets, his department was looking like the fattest crow on the wire. When he was summoned to the top floor, he feared the worst—his own layoff—and expected no less than an order to slash expenses and staff. It was written all over his face.

The top-floor secretaries had been surprised, then, to see him come out of Tom's office a full hour later, practically arm in arm with the CEO. The two had cooked up a plan, and soon enough a memo came out that made it all clear.

Eric's group was being recast as a business unit. It would still serve its sister units, of course, in the way it had done for years. But now, instead of simply cross-charging for expenses incurred, it would charge its "internal customers" according to agreed-upon fees for its marketing services. Such fees would not necessarily reflect actual costs, or even cost-plus pricing. Instead, the new unit would be free to engage in "value pricing" and propose project work essentially the way an outside agency would. The expectation, the memo made clear, was that Eric's group would be more than competitive in its rates; its history of serving the business units would mean no learning curve and low transaction costs. Finally, the memo noted, the marketing group might find opportunities to serve external customers as well, with any excess capacity it had. Fees from such work would help to defray its expenses.

Marketing communications, in short, was now not a cost center but a profit center.

Careful What You Wish For

The reaction to the news was overwhelmingly positive. Any number of Tom's direct reports complimented him on the solution, and their praise seemed genuine. One commented that it was a shrewd way to make Eric come to terms with the cuts he'd inevitably have to make. Others thought a headquarters function that saw them and treated them more like customers than colleagues could only be good.

In fact, it took about two months for the first complaint to crop up. The call came from Andrea Torres, who was looking for five minutes of Tom's time, as soon as he had a break in his schedule. "And what should I say this is in regard to?" O'Reilly's secretary ventured. The answer shot back a little too loudly through the phone: "It's in *regard* to my getting a *bill* from marcom for seventy-five thousand *bucks!*" Eyebrows raised, Grace jotted down Andrea's name and number and told her to be near her phone at 4:10 that afternoon.

The next complaint came just days later. This time it was Sam Jacobs, usually a pretty laid-back fellow. He wasn't so much angry as bewildered. "Are we, uh, not supposed to be going to Eric Palmer's group to get spec sheets and stuff anymore? I need updated materials to hand out at the PROdex show next month, and I don't seem to be getting any response from them."

And there was this complaint from Amanda Black: "I need to talk to Tom about one of Eric Palmer's new *clients*." That last word was laced with derision. "Do you know that he's helping Pandemix come up with better marketing materials? The only problem is, my number one account is Walston Scientific—and Pandemix is its biggest competitor. Walston is not too pleased, as you can imagine. My contact there called me. I didn't even know about it."

Even the administrative staff was affected when it came time to send out the executives' holiday greetings. The cards were always produced by Eric's staff; there was usually an internal contest for all the graphic designers. But this year the form asking secretaries about the quantities they'd need also specified a price and required a charge code. It wasn't huge; just 32 cents a card. Certainly still cheaper than buying cards off the rack, which anyway wouldn't be imprinted with Camden's logo. Still, the suspicion was that the cards probably did not cost that much to produce. It was the talk of the admin meeting that week.

As incident followed incident, Tom was fairly successful at smoothing the ruffled feathers. "It's a new arrangement—give it a chance" was the note he sounded with most of his executives. But the undercurrent of complaint—and the eye rolling and joking in the hallways about marcom's new attitude—continued.

It was hard to reconcile the staff's discontent with the frequent appearances Eric now made in the executive suite, obviously growing more confident in his work. One day, he was waving a letter at Tom, trumpeting the news that his group had just won an award for excellence. Another time, he was showing off the new brochure the communications group had printed to market its services, both inside Camden and outside.

For his part, Tom seemed to be getting an entrepreneurial charge out of hearing about Eric's new business

---

"To look at the two of them," one of the secretaries commented, "you'd think Eric was succeeding beyond Tom's wildest dreams. But how can that be, if everyone else is griping?"

---

and was taking something of a mentoring interest in Eric's career. He'd personally delivered Eric's first external client—a college buddy of Tom's, who owned a small company that made signs for industrial companies. And now, as Eric was explaining how his group would approach the BlinkWare project, Tom was all smiles and nods. "To look at the two of them," one of the secretaries commented, "you'd think Eric was succeeding beyond Tom's wildest dreams. But how can that be, if everyone *else* is griping?"

Time to Rethink Things?

Three weeks passed before Eric popped up on the CEO's radar screen again. The top management team was filtering into the boardroom for its monthly business update while a technician fiddled with the teleconferencing gear to get the rest of the group on the line. Some of the executives had found their seats at the table and were flipping through the spreadsheets that the accounting department had distributed the afternoon before. Others were availing themselves of the bagels and coffee on the sideboard. Buried in their banter was the beginnings of a new gripe.

Apparently, according to the details found deep in accounting's reports, Creative Central, the new name of Eric's group, had sold services to an outside client at a price below actual cost. A couple of the executives had noticed this and were considering making an issue of it during the meeting. "This is ridiculous," one of them said. "I'm paying full price—maybe more—for marketing materials. I keep hearing how busy they are, and meanwhile they're out doing free work for some outfit we don't even have a financial interest in." When

Tom entered the room, the topic shifted. But sure enough, when he emerged from the meeting an hour later, one of the to-dos he'd jotted down was to "sit down with Palmer."

That meeting occurred a few days later, and Eric arrived in his usual high spirits. He'd obviously misread the summons—which was understandable given that the same set of accounting reports had also highlighted his group's growing revenues and margins. When Tom asked him to pull the door shut behind him, and he caught the slight edge in his boss's tone, Eric was instantly confused.

In the corridors, normal office routines carried on—calls were returned, mail was delivered, copies were made, lunch plans were discussed. But anyone wandering near O'Reilly's office door heard a conversation that was building in intensity.

"We're going to have to make some adjustments here," Tom was saying. "It's early days, and we knew we might need to do some rejiggering."

Eric was pushing back. "I don't understand, Tom. I think we're totally on the right track. We're beating plan."

"For one thing, I'm looking at your margins," Tom continued. He was speaking firmly, but not without patience. "The idea was that you'd bill the internal customers fairly to cover the costs of your operation, and in the process they'd become more attuned to the time they were using. But this would indicate you're actually overcharging them."

An indignant Eric shot back: "That's not true. No one's getting fleeced here. As you know, all the units have cut their marketing budgets, so believe me, they're watching every penny. Give us some credit. We're working smarter, and we're also getting some good business from the outside, which is helping boost the margins."

Unknowingly, Eric had just set himself up. Naturally, his boss countered with the evidence from accounting. "Well, it appears those outsiders aren't all paying their way, let alone subsidizing the business units. I see here it cost us $100,000 to get this project done for PRI, and you guys billed them only $80,000."

But Eric recovered quickly enough. He explained that the project at issue was just phase one of a much bigger job. "We knew we were lowballing the bid, but it was an investment. And it's going to pay off, because the client is thrilled with the work." The point seemed to make some sense to Tom, and he shifted back to a more conciliatory tone. He explained that, at the very least, Eric needed to understand that his loss-leader tactic had given additional ammunition to the internal customers who were already complaining.

"They have nothing to complain about!" Eric responded. "I'm not aware of work we've done that our customers wouldn't be proud of. Has anyone said the quality of the work has gone down? Because it hasn't. We've really raised our game. I mean, what about the new recruiting brochure we did for corporate? You said yourself it was first class. And you must love the Web site we did for Scott Milne over in consulting services. That even got a write-up in a trade magazine. Talk to Scott—he's a happy client."

But by now, Tom was losing patience with all the pushback he was getting. Or maybe he was irked at the news that one of his business units had created its own Web site. The units weren't supposed to break ranks from the corporate site unless they had a clear business need. It was the kind of constraint that unit heads chafed under but that Eric's centralized marketing department had always helped to enforce in the past. Both men were speaking loudly now, and others on the floor were becoming aware that there was some kind of issue brewing in the corner office.

"You think no one's complaining?" Tom barked. "Amy Shaughnessy was just up here last week telling me you refused to do a project for her. She's under the impression your group is more interested in doing work for outside clients. You're supposed to be selling your *downtime* to outsiders, not treating our own people like your second priority."

"That project didn't make any sense," Eric shot back. "She couldn't even explain how it fit into any meaningful marketing plan. It's not that we turned down work—we just suggested spending time up front defining the overall strategy of the project. Lacking that, it would just be throwing money down a rat hole to go ahead with that campaign."

Outside the heavy wooden door, O'Reilly's secretary looked up as a delivery boy from the mail room steered his cart off the elevator. At the sound of the arguing voices, he glanced toward Tom's office then shot an inquiring look at Grace. She made a mock grimace, then shrugged her shoulders as she mouthed the name "Eric Palmer."

"Okay, Eric. Come off the high horse," Tom was saying now. "You're not acting like someone who's putting the needs of your internal customers first."

"Fine," came the rejoinder. "And you know what, Tom? Why should I? Because I'll be honest, some of them are my worst customers. We've adopted a whole new attitude toward them, but they've kept the same old attitude toward us. With their other vendors, they wouldn't dream of canceling a meeting at the last minute or failing to meet agreed-upon deadlines. But we're still treated like secretaries."

Eric had crossed a line, and he knew it. He backpedaled some, saying, "I'm sorry, Tom. I just don't get it. You told me I needed to change my mind-set. I needed to manage my department like a business. I needed to be a real entrepreneur. Okay, I've done all that. You told me to run a profit center, and guess what? It's profitable. Why is that a bad thing?" The men's voices were dropping to normal conversational tones. The interest level in the hallway died down, and the meeting was soon over.

Decision Time

It was like clockwork. The evening following an encounter like that one, Tom would stay late in his office, first pacing and fuming, then talking to himself, then dropping into his leather side chair and closing his eyes in deep thought. The day after the encounter, he would take every spare minute between appointments to scribble notes onto a yellow legal pad. The morning of the next day, he would call his secretary in around 9 AM and ask her to get a memo out. This time was no different. It was just before nine Wednesday morning, and Grace had just squeezed a wedge of lemon into a steeping cup of Irish Breakfast tea—Tom's favorite—when her intercom sounded.

But this time, unlike usual, she had no idea what Tom was going to say.

Should Camden Pull the Plug on Its Newest Profit Center?

Four commentators offer expert advice.

➤ Dan Logan

Dan Logan is the president of Trinity Communications, a Boston-based marketing communications firm that focuses on developing brand strategies, creative concepts, and marketing programs for clients.

I've lived this case—I'm probably the closest thing you'll find to a real, live Eric Palmer. Palmer is making three big mistakes—errors that are bad enough to substantiate CEO Tom O'Reilly's withdrawal of his support for the venture.

First, Palmer hasn't designed his services to meet his customers' needs. He thinks they want great creative work, the kind of genius in execution that wins design awards. In reality, they'd be just as appreciative of a marketing professional who presented them with no hassles and did good work that helped them meet their business objectives reliably, on time and on budget. Second, Palmer hasn't spent enough time with his internal customers explaining the new shift from cost-based pricing to value pricing. The two are vastly different.

And Palmer's third mistake is the most harmful: He is focusing on boss satisfaction instead of client satisfaction, a classic error. O'Reilly has seen a lot more of Palmer since this arrangement began. Palmer is frequently popping up to the top floor to get face time and to trumpet his successes. It's clear to me that he's haunting the wrong hallways. He should be spending that time building relationships with his customers.

Is O'Reilly completely blameless in all this? I suppose not. His mistake is imposing this new business arrangement on his organization from the top rather than building widespread consensus and support.

A decade ago, I, too, was running an internal marketing organization, this one at New England Financial. Similarly, I was given the opportunity to turn it into a profit-making business. But my CEO had the wisdom to advise me to gain consensus, convince my internal customers that this arrangement would be advantageous to them, and obtain their support—all of which I'm sure helped me present the proposition positively and head off some of the naysayers.

Senior management also suggested that I develop a detailed business plan projecting revenues and costs for the next three years to demonstrate that I had a reasonable growth strategy. In my case, this was necessary since we were spinning out the business unit formally, not simply creating a new P&L responsibility. My advocates at New England Financial expected at least half of my business to come from external sources after three years. The discipline of a thorough financial analysis and strategic business plan would have been useful to Palmer, too, helping him sharpen his focus as a manager and sell the idea to his colleagues. O'Reilly should have recognized that Palmer would need this and other forms of guidance to transform his mind-set from corporate to entrepreneurial. I'm disinclined, though, to lay much of the blame at O'Reilly's door. He handed Palmer the opportunity of a lifetime, and Palmer did not rise to the occasion.

If I were Palmer, I would immediately go back to those internal clients and eat some humble pie. I'd take responsibility for the problems, and I'd ask for suggestions. If Palmer can capture that feedback formally and make it the basis of a report back to management proposing changes in practices, or possibly a reorganization, he may turn a loss into a gain. He'll need outside clients ultimately, but his business simply won't survive without great referrals from its internal clients. So, if I were him, I'd focus much more on winning and satisfying internal clients than on being aggressive about the outside business.

With the right moves, Palmer can get both. Our own experience at Trinity Communications is the proof. Here we are nine years later, still serving that first client, who now represents a good chunk of our total business. Palmer can probably do the same—but not without a serious shift in his approach. If he isn't willing to do that, O'Reilly should pull the plug.

➤ Michael McKenney

Michael McKenney is the operations manager of
RA Studios/Avid Communications, a business unit of
Rockwell Automation. McKenney is based in Cleveland.

My advice to Tom O'Reilly? Support the business you put in place. Give the marketing communications group time to make this shift from cost center to profit center. O'Reilly has to realize that it's not easy to go from a 100% cost center structure to a fully loaded P&L structure in just a matter of months.

We successfully made this kind of shift with Avid Communications. Our electronic-communications service started out as a business unit of Reliance Electric, a Cleveland-based industrial manufacturing firm. Our department was part of the training unit and was an allocated cost center that created video and multimedia materials for sales, marketing, and training employees at Reliance. When the training unit was threatened with major cost reductions or closure, a team of managers from the graphic arts and video/multimedia groups proposed turning the combined operation into a profit center. The CEO and senior management agreed that such a model would certainly address cost issues—although I really think they had little faith in us succeeding. Their mindset was, "You've been around awhile; we'll give you a year, and then you'll be gone, and the headache will be over." But ultimately we were given the time to set up an infrastructure, develop a brand, and nurture and educate clients internally and externally.

The first year was tough—no sales, no marketing, no advertising; we just opened our doors. Most of our business was still coming from in-house clients. But by the second year, we were turning a profit, and by the mid-1990s, Avid was booking about $2.2 million per year, with half our business coming from internal clients and half from external ones like Lincoln Electric, Marconi, KeyBank, and Cleveland Clinic. This year, we'll probably book close to $5 million in a very difficult business climate. Over the years, we have evolved into a full-service production agency with a staff of 45 at four sites in Ohio and Wisconsin. All that didn't happen overnight. Like Eric Palmer, we've done projects in which we provided much more work than was paid for. (Obviously, we try not to do that often.) But O'Reilly has to realize, as we did, that the company develops client relationships through this process.

On the other hand, Palmer needs to remember the world he grew up in and who's paying his salary. He hasn't been communicating properly or responsibly with his clients and colleagues, forgetting that he must treat them all with respect. As the head of this newly formed profit center, he has to know that he's facing some unique hurdles: External clients will always question your commitment to their projects, figuring you'll drop everything when the parent company comes calling (which is definitely not true). And internal clients will always take you for granted.

It's important to reassure both types of customers. But educating internal business units about the services and value you provide is the most crucial part of making this model work. In the beginning, I can't tell you how many times I heard people say, "You mean other companies actually pay us money for these services? You really do create value?" For us, it took about three years before this change in mind-set happened companywide. But we set the ground rules early: When we first went to the CEO, we said we couldn't have the studio, equipment, or staffers booked with a commercial client and then have him demand access to the studio at the last minute in order to "talk to the troops." This understanding was hammered out at the executive level and communicated down.

The profit center model has proved successful for us. It's kept us fresh and competitive the past 15 years or so. Considering Palmer's early success at attracting business, it sounds like this model could work for Camden Robotics, too—with senior management's support, more effective communication, and clarification of the ground rules for conducting business.

➤ Mark P. Rice

Mark P. Rice is the Murata Dean of the F.W. Olin Graduate School of Business and the Jeffry A. Timmons Professor of Entrepreneurial Studies at Babson College in Wellesley, Massachusetts. He is a coauthor of Radical Innovation: How Mature Companies Can Outsmart Upstarts *(Harvard Business School Press, 2000).*

The question Tom O'Reilly faces is not, "Should Camden Robotics pull the plug on its newest profit center?" It is rather, "Under what conditions will O'Reilly continue to pursue his entrepreneurial experiment with the marketing communications group?" If those conditions can't be met, he needs to determine how he will redirect the venture in order to minimize the negative fallout. To date, the mistakes made have been relatively minor and far outweighed by the positives. But failure to quickly and effectively resolve the conflict arising from these mistakes will doom the new venture.

O'Reilly and Eric Palmer got into this crisis because they made several false business assumptions, the biggest one being that the marcom group would be able to continue to satisfy its internal customers even as it implemented a new pricing strategy for them and aggressively pursued external customers. This is a classic problem for any entrepreneurial venture operating within an established business. The operating principles, organizational culture, and management approach of the new venture are typically different from those of the mainstream business. If those differences aren't managed effectively, mainstream employees can undermine and obstruct the new venture, as they have at Camden.

What should Palmer and O'Reilly do now? Let's start with Palmer. This is not the time for him to protest and risk alienating his champion. So what if he has met or even exceeded the objectives O'Reilly initially established? The CEO is now raising issues that reflect flaws in the initial business model for the marcom group. Responding effectively to mistakes is a key success factor for entrepreneurial ventures. That means recognizing that mistakes are inevitable, making them quickly and inexpensively, learning from them, and adapting the venture's plan and tactics to reflect the lessons.

If Palmer fails to satisfy his internal customers, his venture could be killed. And by not managing those relationships well, he and his team will have to invest an inordinate amount of time and energy in overcoming the negative results of that mismanagement. So instead of objecting, Palmer needs to ask for O'Reilly's help in assessing the situation and deciding how to change his approach.

The CEO bears more of the responsibility for both the problems and the solutions at Camden Robotics. Communication is crucial, but this situation will not be resolved satisfactorily with a memo. This organizational change has stirred up intense negative emotions among Camden's employees, and those feelings need to be acknowledged, defused, and addressed. O'Reilly can start by acknowledging the service problems—with the key internal players individually and collectively—and by taking his share of the blame for creating them. Then he can lead a comprehensive review of the marcom program, seeking to identify what's worked and what hasn't so far. This process should include Palmer, other players within the marketing group, and some of the internal customers who were affected. It will answer fundamental questions about how the marketing group should handle pricing, prioritization of jobs, performance metrics, and so on. It might also help Palmer and his team recognize the importance of serving internal customers effectively.

All the players in this case study need to come to terms with certain trade-offs: strategic versus financial objectives; internal versus external customers; short-term versus long-term performance; and mainstream operations versus entrepreneurial activities. This shared understanding of the trade-offs can then be reflected in a mutually acceptable business model that governs the relationship between the marketing group and its internal customers.

➤ Jeffrey W. Bennett

Jeffrey W. Bennett is a vice president with the management consulting firm Booz Allen Hamilton. He is based in the Cleveland office and focuses primarily on business strategy and organizational issues.

In recognizing the need for a market-like control on Eric Palmer's marketing communications department, Tom O'Reilly was definitely on the right track. But turning the unit from a cost center into a profit center—at least, the way O'Reilly and Palmer implemented the plan—has turned out to be an oversimplified solution, creating headaches for all parties involved. Instead of adopting a profit center structure for the group, O'Reilly should define a role for marcom as a "shared service," creating a more structured relationship between this group and the business units it serves in order to both control costs and ensure quality of service.

Executives face all kinds of thorny issues with cost centers and profit centers. Evaluating service units primarily on whether their costs stay in line with their budgets encourages unit managers to push for more funding and then to make sure to spend every dime as part of building the argument for an even bigger budget the next year. The other units that benefit from these service functions aren't directly exposed to the costs involved, so they tend to lobby for more and better service. This spiraling demand, in turn, bolsters the service units' requests for even bigger budgets. The result is an almost irreconcilable tension between the service functions and the business units they support as to the importance of "what we can afford" versus "functional excellence"—better people, a more consistent corporate look, and so on. With no process in place to resolve this tension, the relationship gets called into question only when outside forces intervene—in this case, the business downturn.

Unfortunately, the move to a profit center creates its own problems, especially if it is implemented in an incomplete way, as appears to be the case at Camden Robotics. Clearly, the move has unleashed previously untapped entrepreneurial energy—witness Palmer's new swagger. But O'Reilly essentially changed the game without clearly defining the rules and boundaries, which has left his other business units in no-man's-land. They have no choice but to go to the existing marcom group for their marketing services, while the marketing group is free to pursue outside clients. O'Reilly shouldn't be surprised to hear from his employees that services have degraded, that prices have increased on the internal transactions where Palmer enjoys a monopoly, and that Palmer has used his position to fund the pursuit of outside business.

O'Reilly could make this internal market complete by letting his business units seek marketing communications services from outside and by spinning off the existing marcom department as an independent unit. If Palmer's group were forced to compete on a level playing field, it would no longer be able to abuse its internal monopoly position. But unless Camden's marketing group has some unique offerings, it may not survive.

Full competition may be theoretically superior to a cost center arrangement, but it may not be the best answer for business functions where the cost of selecting and hiring outside contractors outweighs any improvements in services. This may be particularly true for a function like marketing communications, which often requires industry-specific or even firm-specific expertise.

That brings us back to the notion of shared services, where marcom explicitly exists only to serve Camden's other business units, but within a more structured environment. This will require an explicit charging mechanism so the business units pay only for what they use of this service. Periodically, business units may compare the costs of the marketing services with those of outside suppliers to ensure that they are paying near the market rates. Clearly written service agreements must be drawn up, so the level of expected participation by the service unit is universally understood and can be fairly evaluated by senior management. And the internal customers' satisfaction with the marcom services they are receiving should also be an explicit part of how the group is evaluated.

Originally published in April 2002

Reprint R0204A

SARAH CLIFFE

Can This Merger Be Saved?

Executive Summary

In this fictional case study, a merger that looked like a marriage made in heaven to those at corporate headquarters is feeling like an infernal union to those on the ground.

The merger is between Synergon Capital, a U.S. financial-services behemoth, and Beauchamp, Becker & Company, a venerable British financial-services company with strong profits and an extraordinarily loyal client base of wealthy individuals. Beauchamp also boasts a strong group of senior managers led by Julian Mansfield, a highly cultured and beloved patriarch who personifies all that's good about the company.

Synergon isn't accustomed to acquiring such companies. It usually encircles a poorly managed turnaround candidate and then, once the deal is done, drops a neutron bomb on it, leaving file cabinets and contracts but no people. Before acquiring Beauchamp, Synergon's macho men offered loud assurances that they would leave the tradition-bound company alone—provided, of course, that Beauchamp met the ambitious target numbers and showed sufficient enthusiasm for cross-selling Synergon's products to its wealthy clients.

In charge of making the acquisition work is Nick Cunningham, one of Synergon's more thoughtful executives. Nick, who was against the deal from the start, is the face and voice of Synergon for Julian Mansfield. And Mansfield, in his restrained way, is angry at the constant flow of bureaucratic forms, at the rude demands for instant information, at the peremptory changes. He's even dropping broad hints at retirement. Nick has already been warned: if Mansfield goes, you go.

Six commentators advise Nick on how to save his job by bringing peace and prosperity to the feuding couple.

Nick Cunningham had been against the Beauchamp acquisition from the beginning. Nick's company, Synergon Capital, was a U.S. financial-services behemoth, constantly on the lookout for acquisitions. Typically it acquired turnaround candidates—small companies with established market positions and poor management. But Beauchamp, Becker & Company—a British financial-services company with a great history, strong profits, and an extraordinarily loyal client base of wealthy individuals—didn't fit that description at all.

Nick told his boss, J.J. d'Amato, exactly what he thought. "We'll have to pay too much," he said. "And our cultures are completely different. We don't play the same game. They don't care at all about growth."

J.J. scoffed. "Stop being such a wuss. Let's just do it. I'm sure we can find some money they're leaving on the table." J.J. was rising fast in the company. Listening to subordinates was not among his strengths.

"I'm not so sure," responded Nick. "This isn't a dog that no one wants, run by amateurs. They know more about their customers than we ever will. They're different."

"You worry too much about the soft stuff, Nick," J.J. said. "Relax. We won't force them to change that much. You'll figure out how to make the numbers."

The Synergon Style

Nick had been with Synergon for three years. He'd signed on because of the company's powerhouse performance. Synergon's acquisitions style was legendary. It used a crack team of financial auditors and operations professionals in the due diligence phase to figure out where it could add value. Every team had a "war room" at corporate headquarters with charts, fax machines, computers, and phones. It was staffed around the clock until the deal was done. The team prided itself on identifying every nickel the target business took in or spent.

After Synergon closed a deal, its integration machinery took over. Within weeks, it would close the acquired company's back-office operations and shift work to the nearest Synergon office. Since the acquired company was usually badly managed, Synergon would fire most of the management team within 12 months. Internally, they called this tactic "neutron bombing." The people were gone; only file drawers and contracts remained.

Synergon relished its rough culture. Due diligence teams were called "commando squads"; its members got 18-inch bowie knives with their names and that of the acquired business engraved on them. Negotiating teams got silver-plated sledgehammers if they closed a deal at a price lower than the figure initially quoted to the board. Operating managers who achieved an acquired business's earnings and productivity targets in the first year got 12-inch-long models of a piranha.

Synergon's CEO swore that a "take no prisoners" approach was vital to survival. "The marketplace is war," he told new M.B.A. recruits. "That nickel you see at the end of the negotiation table belongs to us. Get it. It's ours. There may be some collateral damage along the way, but it's our damn nickel."

Sometimes Nick found himself at odds with this culture. It's not that he wasn't competitive, but he had a more thoughtful side than many of his colleagues. He was worried that the Synergon style would someday get in its own way when the company was faced with a situation that didn't fit into its game plan. And Beauchamp, it seemed to him, might be that situation.

A Marriage Made in Heaven

Still, the acquisition made sense. Beauchamp would give Synergon a foothold in Europe—a key part of the company's strategic plan—as well as access to extremely desirable customers. And the deal could make sense from Beauchamp's point of view, too. The company needed to grow, and Synergon had deep pockets, plus some areas of expertise that Beauchamp lacked.

But the acquisition made Nick nervous because it would only work under two conditions: first, if Beauchamp's customers remained happy and, second, if Julian Mansfield, Beauchamp's longtime managing director, stayed on board. Mansfield was smart, sophisticated, and polished. Synergon could learn a lot from how Mansfield managed his clients. The problem was, Synergon didn't think in terms of learning.

Nick pointed out this problem one last time before J.J.'s acquisition pitch to the board, but to no avail. "Let it go, Nick. We're going to jam this through and they're going to love it."

And J.J. was masterful before the board. "We will leave Beauchamp alone. It's a great cross-selling opportunity for us," he said, looking deferentially at Synergon's CEO, Norman Waskewich. "And Nick will help get them focused on growth."

J.J. was on a roll. "Synergon's management and Beauchamp's customers. It's a home run. A slam dunk. They will learn what we've always known: You have to grow or die. They will grow."

Right after the meeting, J.J. set the rules. Pointing a finger directly at Nick, he said, "You have three tasks. One, Beauchamp doubles its earnings in three years.

They need a 20% pop in income in year one. Cut some heads and we'll get there. Two, no blowups at Beauchamp. Nada. The press and the analysts are all over us on this deal. Third, I want their big customers so I can pitch our products. And I want Mansfield to get me in. If he walks, they walk, and our pitch walks. If Mansfield walks, you walk out right behind him. Got it?"

The Venerable Beauchamp

Soon after the deal closed, Nick made a quick trip to London. He met briefly with Julian Mansfield and the rest of the senior management team. There was a lot of polite talk about Beauchamp's wonderful traditions and the "significant synergies" that existed between the two companies, but not much of substance occurred.

Nick scheduled a second trip for a month later—he was facing the end of Synergon's fiscal year and couldn't get back any sooner. In spare moments during the ensuing weeks, he studied Beauchamp. The place was impressive, no doubt about it. Beauchamp was an unusually stable company. Its management team consisted of 16 people who'd worked together for more than a decade. The 700 associates routinely shifted from one project team to another to handle a surge in business, solve a customer problem, or get a product to market. The turnover rate was a mere 4%, and managers averaged 21 years of experience with the company. (In contrast, Synergon's turnover rate was 21%, and the average tenure for managers was 6 years.)

Julian Mansfield presided over the whole like an old-fashioned patriarch. His title was managing director, but he *was* Beauchamp. He was the godfather of dozens of associates' children. He was revered within the company for his business sense and character, and he was well known in charity circles for his generosity.

As Nick was pondering his second face-to-face meeting with Mansfield, the Synergon integration team swung into action. First, Synergon's HR director informed his counterpart at Beauchamp that Beauchamp's Associate Bonus Plan, which provided every associate with at least a modest bonus, would be scrapped. Synergon's Big Bang Bonus Plan, which favored senior managers who achieved high earnings growth, would take its place. The change would reduce the bonus for 70% of Beauchamp's associates.

Second, Synergon closed the cafeteria that for years had provided Beauchamp employees with a free lunch. Employees complained to one another as they ran out at lunchtime for take-out food. Julian was mortified that the "caf ladies," who'd been with Beauchamp for years, were let go with only a minimal severance package.

Third, Synergon's finance director informed his counterpart that purchasing and travel would now go through Synergon vendors. Agreements with vendors in these areas were geared toward big-ticket items, such as executive office furniture or cross-Atlantic airfare. Although Synergon's arrangements kept its own costs down, they were bound to push Beauchamp's up, since the smaller firm used regional carriers with lower local fares. People at Beauchamp were upset that long-standing relationships with local suppliers would be eliminated.

To top it all off, Synergon was now requiring multiple approvals before granting customer credit; the approvals would be based on customer industry, contract profitability, customer location, and the type of asset offered as collateral. Beauchamp salespeople had always made credit decisions with a conversation and a handshake. Under the new regime, Beauchamp received its first customer complaint in living memory when a valued customer of many years lost a deal while waiting for his loan approval to come through.

Julian and his longtime executive assistant, Olivia Carlton, heard daily complaints, too, about the new reports and forms that Beauchamp managers had to fill out for Synergon officials, who never introduced themselves or explained why the forms were necessary. Synergon was asking for numbers on market share, competitor data, cost reductions, productivity increases, and risk allocation.

When direct communication did take place, it was horrible. The day before Nick's second visit, a Synergon financial auditor brought Olivia to tears. "Fax me the F-14 sheet in the next hour or I will be in your face

Monday morning and your boss will hear about it. *Get me my report.*"

The Honeymoon's Over

When Nick walked into Julian's office on his second visit, the older man rose and shook hands, trying to be cordial, but he was clearly annoyed. After some initial small talk, he said to Nick, "Let me ask you a question. Is Synergon *trying* to offend me?"

"Goodness, no," said Nick, taken aback. "What do you mean?"

"Well, you can see that I'm not a small man," answered Julian. (Indeed, he was well over six feet tall.) "As you know, I travel a great deal, and I happen to suffer from arthritis. Yet my assistant has just informed me that I'm not to fly business class to Paris. Company policy doesn't *allow* that without permission from my superior. That would be you, I expect . . . ?"

Nick stuttered out an explanation and assured Julian that the policy would be overridden. Julian gazed out the window for a long moment, then turned back to Nick.

"Look, Mr. Cunningham, we can help you reach these absurdly high target numbers you've set, but not unless you let us do our work."

"What do you mean?" responded Nick, genuinely puzzled.

"I'll show you what I mean," said Julian, opening his desk drawer and pulling out a two-inch pile of faxes. "These are just a few of the vital, urgent, ASAP messages we've received from your people. Do you have any idea how time-consuming and idiotic these forms are?"

Nick recognized most of them. Some were administrative: the travel center asking whether the "new employee" would prefer nonsmoking hotel rooms and what kind of airplane seat, aisle or window.

Some were procedural: HR asking that performance evaluations be completed for all subordinates in SEPR format—which meant Synergon Employee Performance Review, but there was no explanation. And the S-EEO-1, which asked Beauchamp to classify employees by race, gender, and level, something not done in the United Kingdom.

Some were financial: the B-52s, growth projections for the next three years, and the M-16s, cost-reduction sheets for the past 12 months.

All told, several dozen requests from 14 different people at corporate. Nick recognized this as routine work that Synergon managers did at home on Sunday afternoons.

"I'll do my best," replied Nick. "I can get someone over here to help you out. But this is how we operate."

Mansfield narrowed his eyes and said with barely concealed anger, "I'm sure it is how you operate. But if your operations mean that my company—which was ticking along very nicely, thank you—becomes paralyzed, then we both have a problem. You people have a very odd notion of what 'leaving Beauchamp alone' means."

After a brief pause, he went on. "You know, Mr. Cunningham, you seem like a nice fellow. But I've been around too long to have to put up with this much impertinence. To have these boys you call auditors insulting my assistant is, frankly, something I can do without. My wife's been on at me to retire for the last year or two and, I must say, that idea is starting to sound attractive.

"I have a suggestion. Why don't you take the rest of the day off? You can get over your jet lag. There's a Sargent exhibition at the Tate that you might enjoy, and Miss Carlton could probably get you some theater tickets for tonight, if you like. Why don't we meet tomorrow morning, after you've slept on it, to talk about the future of the company."

Can the Beauchamp Acquisition Be Salvaged? How Should Nick Prepare for Tomorrow's Meeting with Julian?

Six commentators explain how Nick can bring peace and prosperity to the newly merged companies.

➤ Bill Paul

Bill Paul is a partner in DelTech Consulting, a firm that special-izes in acquisitions integration. It is based in Avon, Connecticut.

Nick Cunningham's problem is that Synergon excels at assimilating new companies but is terrible at integrating them. Between the two tasks lies a world of difference.

Assimilation works when the goal of the acquisition is to consolidate the two companies. In such cases, the deal itself is the major work. Once the deal has gone through, the objective is simple: make the acquired company just like the purchaser. In some cases, a consolidating acquisition means isolating a tangible asset, product line, or high-performing unit and forgetting the rest. In any event, the acquired company's organizational culture doesn't matter, because it likely caused the underperformance that led to the acquisition. The same is true for that company's people. Their only choice is to adapt or leave.

Assimilation does not work in the case of a strategic acquisition, joint venture, or merger—integration is required instead. The real work begins after the deal. The goal is either to create a wholly new third company or to maintain separate identities while sharing strengths. The acquired company changes some practices, keeps others, and transfers still others to the purchaser. Organizational culture is critical, and people are paramount—the purchaser should retain most of the acquired company's employees.

Acquiring organizations are inclined to force assimilation on their new companies, regardless of circumstances. After a deal, many well-intentioned people will inundate the acquired company with requests and changes in an attempt to improve its business performance or its connections with the new parent. The result is an "accumulation effect" in which each request is modest in its own right, but the totality paralyzes the acquisition. Over time, this effect erodes the behaviors that made the company a success. That's exactly what is happening in this case. Beauchamp requires integration, and Nick needs to override Synergon's usual assimilation tactics.

In the short term, Nick should appoint an on-site integration manager from Synergon. Beauchamp doesn't know who or what is important, so every request appears serious, even the F-14 sheet from the financial auditor, who may be a first-year associate trying to impress the bosses. Beauchamp has no idea whether the form needs attention today or next week—or perhaps it can be stored in the circular file? The Synergon integration manager would know.

Nick then needs to drive a strategy that applies the three C's of integration: clarity, conflict resolution, and consensus building.

Nick must identify and clarify the "nonnegotiables" of the deal. Those are mainly the financial targets that led Synergon to make the acquisition. They include increasing Beauchamp's net income by 20% in the first year, doubling it in three years, and reducing the head count. Other nonnegotiables would include adhering to Synergon's risk-assessment process and introducing Beauchamp's customers to Synergon.

Nick also needs to clarify the differences between the businesses and why those differences exist. When you tamper with a business without understanding why it is successful, you confuse people in the acquired company and risk destroying its value. When two organizations are of equal size, such misunderstanding results in cultural wars that make it impossible to realize financial goals; consider the deal involving AT&T and NCR. And if the purchaser is much larger, the acquired company's strengths are usually trampled on. That's what happened when Quaker Oats bought Snapple, and that's what's happening in this case.

Nick can still prevent the misunderstandings from ending in disaster. To build consensus, he should bring the key people from both sides together for a couple of days. In-depth discussions will allow the two companies' executives to gain an appreciation of their different places in the market and different approaches to doing business. Having done that, the two sides should come to an understanding—based on available data and customer research—about what the market demands are likely to be over the next couple of years. If Synergon and Beauchamp build a business model based on the connections between market demands, competitive advantages, and organizational processes, they will be able to resolve organizational conflicts.

This group meeting is essential. If Nick fails to bring the two sides together around market demands, people will try to resolve problems one at a time, the integration process will drag on, and the acquisition will suffer. In another scenario, conflicts will simply be resolved on the basis of power or politics. In other words, Synergon will win every battle but destroy the reason for the deal.

Once a broad consensus has been reached, it will be possible for Julian Mansfield to talk about specific difficulties. For example, he may contend that Beauchamp will not be able to double its net income in three years and abide by Synergon's risk process. The reason? Competitors will poach customers by offering a quick turnaround on financing. Synergon's managers may disagree, but at least the two sides will be able to have a reasonable discussion.

One last note: before any of this can work, Nick needs to get Mansfield on his side. He needs to empathize with him and express personal regret about how the transition process has gone so far. In return, he needs a commitment from Mansfield that he will stay on and help Nick with the transition. If these two men can begin to understand each other, they may be able to salvage the acquisition.

➤ J. Brad McGee

J. Brad McGee is a senior vice president at Tyco International, the conglomerate based in Exeter, New Hampshire.

Our assets wear shoes." I first heard that expression from the CEO of a service-based company while I was in the diligence phase of acquiring her business. She was referring to the people-oriented nature of service companies—their reliance on relationships and the unique skills of individuals. In this case, she was advising me to be cautious about unraveling the fabric that held her people together. The same cautionary words apply to Synergon's acquisition of Beauchamp.

Clearly, this acquisition is a departure for Synergon. Its success depends not solely on reducing costs but also on increasing revenues. That's difficult for two reasons. First, selling incremental products to the same customers requires that they change their behavior. Second, it's hard to forecast increased revenues accurately; forecasts in this case would be susceptible to exaggeration. Nonetheless, this acquisition can be saved.

I've been involved in dozens of acquisitions, and in my experience there's always room for improvement—even when a company is well managed. I recommend that Nick do the following:

Make Julian Mansfield part of the solution, not the problem. Mansfield has already expressed his willingness to help Synergon reach its "absurdly high" target numbers. At least for the short term, Nick should leave Mansfield clearly in charge of Beauchamp and allow him to create and own the plan to realize Synergon's targets. He likely performed his own diligence on Synergon before the merger and understood their financial goals. He also likely gave his blessing to the merger knowing that he would be under Synergon's management.

Put Mansfield on an attractive P&L-based incentive program. If Mansfield is a good manager, he will use the new tools available to him to drive both revenue gains and cost reductions based on the aggressive P&L targets. Those tools include access to a broader range of products and to Synergon's ideas about streamlining operations. Large cost-reduction opportunities can exist even in well-managed companies that are acquired. A well-structured incentive plan could be all Beauchamp needs. At the end of the day, does it matter how Mansfield achieves the targets?

Put a finance person from Synergon into Beauchamp. Make sure that the CFO or corporate controller at Beauchamp is a person who knows Synergon. The importance of this action cannot be overstated. Having such a person in place offers two advantages: it establishes an insider who can monitor Beauchamp's financial health, its progress toward meeting goals, and its organizational dynamics; and it gives Mansfield direct access to knowledge about how he should be integrating the two firms. Finance people often work well in this role. They are generally viewed as nonthreatening and often have a good understanding of business operations.

Closely monitor Mansfield's performance. Due diligence can be very good at identifying the financial, legal, and environmental fitness of an acquisition target. However, it often fails to uncover the interpersonal dynamics that hold service companies together. In this case, it's difficult to assess how critical Mansfield is to Beauchamp's continued success. Nick should use the first three to six months after the merger as an evaluation period (the finance person is critical to this phase). After that, it should be clear whether or not Synergon needs to keep Mansfield on board.

Back off the bureaucracy. Synergon's bureaucracy will only burden Beauchamp, and it may prove demoralizing.

Now to the more immediate concern in this case: the upcoming meeting between Nick and Julian. Nick should brief J.J. d'Amato on the plan of action detailed above and have d'Amato recommend a financial person to bring into Beauchamp. Nick should think through the plan and be able to discuss it clearly and provide supporting arguments for each part of the plan.

During the meeting, he should assure Mansfield that he will be in charge of achieving the aggressive targets for Beauchamp and that he will be enriched for meeting or exceeding those goals. At the same time, he must inform Mansfield of the ways Synergon can help him, and he must get Mansfield to agree to include a Synergon financial person on his management team.

The meetings I've had of this type have gone very smoothly. Although people are often reluctant to change, they also realize—whether they say so or not—that being acquired means relinquishing ownership and control of their company.

➤ Jill Greenthal

Jill Greenthal is a managing director of Donaldson, Lufkin, and Jenrette in New York City. She was the lead investment banker for TCI in its merger with AT&T.

The senior management team at Synergon knew that they needed to "leave Beauchamp alone." But somehow that idea was forgotten after the deal went through. Nick's task now is to build a constituency within Synergon to treat the Beauchamp acquisition differently. It won't be easy, because Synergon's leaders have a playbook approach to acquisitions, and they've been very successful with it. This time, though, they've bought a good business, not a broken one, and they need to recognize that.

They also need to recognize—through actions, not lip service—that they've bought a company driven by the personality of its senior managers, especially Julian Mansfield. The problem is, Beauchamp's senior people probably made a fair amount of money from the sale, and it's going to be hard for Synergon to enlist the aid and support of people it's just made financially comfortable. Many acquiring companies recognize this problem in the deal structure and pay senior management over two to three years, as goals are met. If Synergon has failed to consider this issue, it should move fast and put in place some very large incentives to get Mansfield and members of his senior management team to stay.

Next, Synergon needs to rethink the mechanics of integration. It can't leave Beauchamp completely alone, but neither should it take over every aspect of the business. It has to find a balance. For example, Synergon has a legal responsibility to understand Beauchamp's numbers, its financial reporting, and its credit risks. But other areas, such as purchasing and employee benefits, can be left to Beauchamp's discretion. Matters aren't helped by the condescending attitude drifting across the Atlantic from corporate headquarters. That attitude indicates that Synergon believes it has taken on another broken company and is prepared to demolish the old structure and build an entirely new one.

So far, Nick hasn't really done his job. There are, however, several steps he can take to avert a meltdown. Essentially, Nick must serve as—or appoint—a referee who will make the integration work by helping the two companies understand each other.

To accomplish that goal, he needs to persuade people on both sides to think in new ways. He must convince the people at Synergon headquarters that the acquisition will fail unless certain rules are broken—that, for example, not all the company's forms are critical to Beauchamp's future success. And he needs to be Mansfield's advocate at the top levels of the company. He's the only one who can absorb Mansfield's concerns and translate them effectively.

In the meantime, he should reassure Mansfield at their next meeting that he will work on Beauchamp's behalf to reduce the bureaucratic irritations now plaguing the company. Then he should turn to the serious matter of making the numbers. It's a hopeful sign that Mansfield seems to understand the objectives and has even indicated that Beauchamp can meet Synergon's "absurdly high" target numbers.

It's critical that Mansfield agree to cross-sell Synergon's products. That's not going to happen unless it's in the financial interests of Beauchamp's associates, including

Mansfield. Nick and Julian need to map out a sound game plan that includes changes in compensation, cross-selling incentives, and an understanding about how to retain customers and employees. If Beauchamp's employees have not been granted stock in Synergon, that omission should be corrected.

During these conversations, it will be important for Nick to convey to Mansfield what he needs to do to become part of the corporate team. At the same time, they need to start planning for Mansfield's eventual retirement. Should they look to the next layer at Beauchamp? Or should they bring people in from Synergon to learn the business? This issue needs to be addressed sooner rather than later.

If Nick can persuade Synergon's top management not to fix what ain't broke, and if he can hold Mansfield's hand a little while the integration phase moves forward, then Beauchamp's future has a chance to be a happy marriage of growth and tradition.

➤ Dale Matschullat

Dale Matschullat is vice president and general counsel for Newell Company in Freeport, Illinois; he oversees the company's acquisition integrations.

In my experience, it is easier to do a job yourself than to manage others who are trying to do it. The Synergon story suggests that my experience is valid.

If I were meeting with Julian Mansfield, I would start by telling him that I appreciate his signing on to Synergon's budgetary goals. I would let him know that, although we must agree on budgetary and strategic goals, he will ultimately be in charge of reaching them.

Next, I would ask Mansfield to develop a strategic plan for the business. The plan should be reviewed at least annually and must include: an analysis of the marketplace; an assessment of competitors' strengths and a plan for exploiting their weaknesses; suggestions for building on Beauchamp's strengths and attacking its weaknesses; a discussion of strategic opportunities; and a plan to make cross-selling effective. The strategic plan should contain virtually no numbers.

I would also ask Mansfield to prepare a budget for the next operating year—a nuts-and-bolts document that commits the company to figures for sales and profits. It will be negotiated with me and others at Synergon and must be based on a realistic sales forecast. Once the terms have been agreed on, they have to be met.

It is important that Mansfield's team develop these documents. As long as Mansfield can sell his vision to Synergon, he will shape the future of Beauchamp. Synergon has the capital to make his vision real.

Further, I would discuss the huge dissonance between the corporate cultures. I would tell Mansfield that I am going to bring a high-level Synergon manager into Beauchamp— probably a corporate controller. The controller, who will be a member of Beauchamp's senior management team, will handle inside operations and manage costs. Mansfield will be free to manage sales growth and customer relationships. He and the controller will meld the two cultures.

All those ASAP messages from Synergon will go directly to the new controller. If there are problems, I would tell Mansfield this: "Not only will I be your boss, I will be your shield. You are responsible for Beauchamp's success, and as long as you respond successfully, you will be left to run it. It is my job to see to that."

I would then focus on Mansfield's hints about retirement. Optimally, Mansfield should run Beauchamp. But it is unacceptable for him to manage the integration with his mind on retirement. I would remind him that Synergon paid a premium for Beauchamp, partly because of its respect for his accomplishments. Synergon believes that he has the vision, guts, experience, and stamina to grow the company. However, unless Mansfield is 100% behind the endeavor, Synergon will not provide the capital he needs to do it.

Mansfield has to understand that Synergon, in its brash way, brings important principles to the table. It is very profit oriented and believes in lean, decentralized organizations that are self-driven but accountable.

So if Mansfield wants to fly business class around Europe, I will support it. But his strategic plan is going to require substantial growth. Perhaps he would prefer to fly coach and spend the savings on another design engineer. Such trade-offs are his to make, but he is accountable.

And yes, we can phase in the Synergon bonus plan. But at Synergon, bonuses are an important part of the compensation scheme. They are awarded when the budgeted numbers have been achieved. They are not given out for any other reason. Mansfield will have to find a way to motivate Beauchamp's midlevel associates without a bonus plan.

If Mansfield agrees to implement the ideas outlined in this meeting, Synergon will have purchased Beauchamp on the cheap.

➤ Daniel Vasella

Daniel Vasella is president of Novartis, the company that resulted from the merger of Ciba Geigy and Sandoz. It is based in Basel, Switzerland.

Nick's not in an easy position. He has to manage a merger he doesn't believe in. His supervisor either does not understand or does not care about the cultural issues separating the companies being merged. And he's overseeing an acquired company whose managing director has been highly successful, is close to retirement, and has no incentive to change.

Nick has two choices. He can impose Synergon's culture—its strategy, business processes, and people—on Beauchamp. Or he can help Julian Mansfield find a way to operate in a reasonable environment. The first choice isn't really viable: Mansfield will leave, Nick will be fired, and the acquisition will fail. So Nick needs to ensure that he and Mansfield come to an understanding.

Nick should go into tomorrow's meeting with a crisis-management mind-set. He must stabilize the situation. He needs to get Mansfield's agreement to corrective actions, as well as his commitment to stay for at least six months. I suggest six months because I don't believe Mansfield would commit to staying longer at this stage. Once Nick has established that he's acting in good faith, he may be able to negotiate a longer-term commitment with Mansfield at a later date.

I propose that he do the following. First, he needs to recognize the tremendous past achievements of Mansfield and Beauchamp and establish a sense of mutual respect. Second, he needs to depict in a compelling way Beauchamp's opportunity to become Synergon's flagship European operation. Mansfield has to buy in to a common future that is better in some ways than Beauchamp's past. Third, Nick has to explain Synergon's original motives for the acquisition—not only to get a foothold in Europe but also to introduce Synergon's products to Beauchamp's customers. I'm not sure that Mansfield ever understood these things. Fourth, Nick must acknowledge the existing problems and his own responsibility for them. He should find out which problems are the most disturbing and require immediate correction, and how Mansfield would go about mending these problems. That is, Nick needs to tap Julian's experience and, in so doing, acknowledge his capabilities. It's important that he act quickly.

Further, Nick should talk not just with J.J. d'Amato but also with Synergon's CEO. This is a major acquisition; there's a lot of money at stake. He should request formal approval for corrective actions. For example, there should be a commitment that all requests from the United States be cleared through him. And if Julian has never met Synergon's CEO, Nick should arrange a meeting.

Finally, to tie up the loose ends of the short-term crisis, Nick should propose biweekly progress reviews, to be conducted either by phone or in person. The sum of these steps should prevent the short-term problems from leading to a total deterioration of the acquisition.

In the long term, you're left with the question of how you align two companies with totally different cultures. For example, I do not think that Beauchamp is well suited to grow Synergon in Europe. I would rather relocate one or two Synergon people and put them under Mansfield; they would be responsible for growing the business externally.

What are the lessons of this case? When you make an acquisition, you must have total agreement on the merger objectives and key strategies. You must share a vision of the value added by the merger. You have to be aware of cultural differences. Eventually, the customer base, the strategy, and the culture of the acquired company have to fit. And once you have a common understanding of the merger objectives and key strategies, you have to gain rapid agreement on responsibilities, accountability, empowerment, and boundaries—and you have to keep the lines of communication open.

➤ Albert J. Viscio

Albert J. Viscio is a vice president of Booz-Allen & Hamilton in San Francisco. He has consulted extensively on postmerger integration.

Synergon has made errors in both the mechanical integration and the strategic value integration of its new acquisition.

The mechanical integration is not being tailored to the situation. Instead, Synergon is using its standard integration process. Some of J.J. d'Amato's guidance has turned out to be just plain wrong. Cutting heads backfired. And the efficiencies being introduced aren't really efficiencies—Beauchamp's spending more on the airlines, for example.

Nobody ever clarified what "leaving Beauchamp alone" meant. It was Nick's job to do that. It was misleading to say "We'll leave you alone" and then close the cafeteria. Beauchamp didn't feel left alone. Synergon has created a very poor foundation for any kind of strategic integration.

This acquisition was about adding strategic value to both firms; it wasn't about cost reductions. But nobody seems to be talking about how strategic value will be added—and it doesn't happen automatically. Nick needs an answer to the question, What will the Synergon-owned Beauchamp look like? It's apparent that there is potential—Beauchamp needs to grow and Synergon wants wealthy European customers. But those mutual needs don't seem to be a focus of the integration effort. They should be. They're the whole point.

Three elements have been lacking: vision, architecture, and leadership.

Synergon never developed a vision of what Beauchamp could be. The old model wasn't right: Beauchamp wasn't growing. Pulling it into the Synergon fold isn't working either. Nobody's put forth a new value proposition for customers. Without that, you don't have a company.

As far as we know, nobody's talked about architecture: How does Beauchamp fit into Synergon? How are the companies related? What's the process for cross-selling going to be? Synergon's tried-and-true integration mechanisms need to be tailored, probably radically.

Finally, Nick has abdicated his leadership responsibilities. He should have been working with Mansfield and the other Beauchamp senior managers on creating a shared vision and common values. But he hasn't spent much time on the ground with these people. They've been bothered with forms but not graced with his physical presence. Nick should be identifying and building leadership prospects from within Beauchamp's ranks—forming partnerships and building excitement about the company's future.

So Nick has a big problem: a derailed acquisition. He should go to that show tonight. Then he should find a way to reach common ground on a vision that will excite both Mansfield and Synergon's CEO. He needs to develop a process for getting there based on the understanding that value is going to be found in the market, not in cost savings.

He needs to find people at Beauchamp who will help lead that change process, and he probably needs to do battle with his own management. It's important that he talk to

Mansfield and take responsibility for the many problems that have hurt the acquisition.

Having said all this, I have to point out that when a deal's success is contingent on retaining a senior person, it usually fails. We've done some research in order to understand why, and the answer is quite straightforward. When we asked top people why they'd moved on after a merger, they said, very simply, that they had no reason to stay.

Let's face it: when you acquire a company and neutron bomb it, you don't risk much because you don't need its people. But if the company's value lies in its customer relationships, you have to keep your finger off the button and think instead about the harder process of persuading the people you've acquired to work toward the company's goals.

Originally published in January–February 1999
Reprint R99103

What's He Waiting For?

Executive Summary

The powerful division heads at Captiva Corporation had high expectations for Doug Yacubian when he signed on as the food and beverage company's first chief operating officer. But a year later, they're joking caustically that Doug still hasn't figured out what he's supposed to be doing there.

Yacubian was a rising star before he came to Captiva in this fictional case study. At Marcella International, he had helped build a widely successful line of beverages into a solidly profitable global presence. By all external measures, he was well suited to become the hands-on COO that Captiva had needed ever since CEO Peter Tyler became less interested in day-to-day operations.

Executive Summary

In Doug's first week, several customers suffered food poisoning because of a formulation error at a Captiva plant. Yacubian offered to do interviews with the trade press and meet with U.S. distributors to help quell the crisis, but after it was decided that Tyler should take those actions himself, Yacubian "folded his tent," as one division head puts it.

The recall crisis was followed by a hostile tender offer, which occupied the company's top executives for six months. By the time Yacubian drafted a proposal for reorganization of corporate responsibilities, division heads and at least one director had grown impatient with him. At a retreat for the board and management, the directors asked him point blank: "What's taking you so long?"

Yacubian, frustrated, tells his father that it's been a long time since he felt this incompetent. What went wrong at Captiva? Four commentators offer their opinions and advice.

The ride back to the airport from Captiva Corporation's annual retreat for the board and top management was proceeding slowly. Cynthia Speedwell and Ben Esperanza sat glumly in the backseat of their limo, checking their watches and making contingency plans in case they missed their flights home. Ben grumbled to his friend and fellow Captiva division president, "At this rate, by the time we get to the airport, Doug Yacubian might actually have figured out what he's supposed to do as Captiva's COO."

Cynthia replied with mock horror, "Do you really think it'll take more than a year to get to the airport?" They snickered. But then Cynthia grew serious. After a pause, she said, "You know, I *am* surprised Yacubian hasn't taken charge of anything yet. I guess the board's getting uncomfortable, too. Why on earth hasn't Peter off-loaded anything to him?"

It had been almost a year since Doug Yacubian had been named COO of Captiva. Hired as a hands-on complement to the company's strategy-oriented CEO—and as a source of new entrepreneurial energy—Doug appeared to have accomplished little in that year. The great expectations that had accompanied his arrival had faded away like the fizz in a soft drink. Board

---

Hired as a hands-on complement to Captiva Corporation's strategy-oriented CEO—and as a source of entrepreneurial energy—COO Doug Yacubian appeared to have accomplished little in his first year.

---

members and others at Captiva were growing increasingly impatient with him.

Before being recruited by Captiva, Doug had been a rising star at Marcella International, where in less than five years he had helped Jack Marcella build the wildly successful BrewHeaven beverage business from a vague concept into a solidly profitable global presence. At Marcella, Doug had managed teams, divisions, and facilities. He had successfully consolidated disparate internal functions into a well-coordinated whole as BrewHeaven grew. However, after the Marcella family announced the impending sale of its company to Drinkmasters, a U.K.-based conglomerate, he began to look elsewhere. He was highly regarded throughout the food and beverage industry: he knew the intricacies of developing global brands and was considered a skilled inside player. By all external measures, he was well suited to the number two job at Captiva.

After the search firm approached him on behalf of Captiva, he had several in-depth conversations with president and CEO Peter Tyler and the other members of the search committee. Ultimately, the decision was easy for both sides: the opportunity at Captiva seemed ideal to Doug, and Doug seemed ideal to the search committee.

Captiva Corporation Under Peter Tyler

Tyler, while not a flamboyant leader, was viewed as yet another of the transformative CEOs for which Captiva had been known since its founding as a cheese producer nearly a century ago. All of Captiva's CEOs had believed that what had worked well for the company in the past was unlikely to work well in the future and had seen it as their responsibility to foster change. As a result, Captiva developed a knack for reinventing itself, both internally and in the eyes of its customers.

Under Tyler's leadership, the transformation of Captiva meant the addition of several prominent brands that lent themselves well to globalization. In the first years of his tenure, Captiva consisted of three major divisions—dairy products, poultry, and prepared foods. Captiva then began to expand aggressively, acquiring prominent brand names in frozen foods, juices, and bakery goods. While people joked that the mild-mannered CEO "never met a brand he didn't like," they had great respect for his judgment in picking brands that would be successful and complement Captiva's other lines.

But as Captiva's brand portfolio expanded, Tyler became far less interested in the day-to-day operations of the corporation. His hands-off approach created a need for a new executive position at a senior corporate level. The powerful division presidents, who reported to Tyler, were among the most vocal in articulating the need for a peer who would manage internal operations. Organizational-design consultants developed a job description for the COO with the help of senior managers, the board, and Tyler.

The description, written in broad language, stated that the COO would gradually take over the management of corporate functions such as human resources and finance and administration and would eventually oversee some of the brands. It also said the COO would rationalize in-house manufacturing capacity and monitor the installation of an enterprisewide information system. The job description didn't suggest in any way that the COO might succeed Tyler, whose retirement was at least 15 years off.

After it became clear that there were no suitable internal candidates, an executive search firm helped recruit Doug. He came across well in the interviews, providing decisive answers to questions on how he would tackle the COO job and on the pace of change he considered appropriate. Doug responded to many questions with a prefatory comment: "This reminds me of a situation we had at BrewHeaven." The search committee noted privately that the situations were not analogous—Marcella was not much like Captiva—yet committee members did feel that his answers were conceptually sound. It seemed to them that he'd bring some of BrewHeaven's entrepreneurial flair to Captiva's internal organization.

Tyler's job description didn't change when the COO role was created, but many senior managers, the board, and Tyler himself assumed that he would delegate substantial responsibility to Doug. During the meeting at which the search committee decided to make Doug an offer, Peter said, "The transition should be pretty smooth, given this guy's eagerness to make a difference and to do so sooner rather than later."

A Tough Start

So it was with high hopes that Captiva brought Doug aboard in the third week of June. Unfortunately, during that week, the biggest crisis in the company's history exploded in the headlines. Because of a formulation error at one of Captiva's manufacturing plants, several customers suffered severe food poisoning. Captiva immediately recalled a whole line of products and mounted a huge PR campaign aimed at salvaging the brand. Since this occurred during Doug's first week on the job, he couldn't do much to help manage the crisis. Besides, Peter's was the public face of Captiva; it would have been inappropriate for anyone but Peter Tyler to have been in control.

"The timing wasn't great for Yacubian, what with the product recall and everything," Ben Esperanza said as the limo inched off the interstate and onto the airport road. "But he could have been more active even so. Remember when he offered to do interviews with the trade press? Then visit the U.S. distributors in an effort to keep them happy? Those were good ideas, but once they were on the table, it seemed like Peter should do them. After that, Yacubian sort of folded his tent."

"I don't know," said Cynthia. "It's not like he could have done an 'I'm in charge here' in his first week. Hell, he and Peter probably hadn't sat down even once before that crisis erupted. It took the better part of four months to bring it to a conclusion. And the rest of the year's been a little hairy, too. Still, they don't seem to be making much progress, do they?"

Ben shook his head. He added, "You know, Cynthia, you're one of the few people who could actually push Tyler and Yacubian to get their act together. I bet they'd both listen to you. You've been around for so long, and you were instrumental in hiring Doug."

Meanwhile . . .

In the back of another car bound for the airport, Doug Yacubian was talking on a cell phone with his father, a retired corporate lawyer. "I don't know what they expected. One of the board members got on my case at the retreat. Said he thought I'd be playing a more active role by now. I said I thought enough dust had settled for that to happen, finally. I glanced over at Peter Tyler—who looked totally sheepish—and he nodded. The board member shook his head and said, 'Well, what's taking you so long?'

"I reminded him, as gently as I could, that after the recall crisis, Peter took three weeks off. Then came the fire drill of the fourth quarter, which occupied everyone's attention, especially since the recall threatened the entire year's earnings. Then came the hostile tender offer. Peter and I couldn't very well say, 'Hey, let's do all the organizational changes even though we're in the midst of fighting off a tender offer,' could we? That took another six months or so."

His father interrupted him. "Did you remind him that you weren't just twiddling your thumbs? You tried to take on some firefighting responsibilities in the recall crisis, but Tyler decided it was more his role to play. And you told me a few weeks ago that you felt good about how the ERP installation was going. Plus you've been closing down manufacturing plants, right? Did you point that out?"

"Nah," replied Doug. "The guy was already looking at me like I was making excuses, so I just kept quiet."

Doug's father laughed sardonically. "I guess you'd sound like you were whining if you told them how hard they made it for you to get up and running at first. Remember those problems you had with your e-mail and your computer? The integration support was lousy. Your assistant knew even less than you did about the place."

Doug chuckled. "Peter knows all that. When I first came on board, he told me not to expect too much the first year: it was about building relationships, learning the ropes—buying a house, even! And he seems comfortable with my performance when we do talk. But the people around me, and the board, don't seem to get that impression from him.

The frustrating thing is, I'd been planning to talk with Tyler about reorganizing corporate responsibilities right after we got back. In fact, I'd drafted a proposal right before we left for this blessed off-site. I should have talked it through with him before we got here. It would have saved both of us some embarrassment today. Now it's going to look like I wrote the plan in response to the director's complaint."

Both men were quiet for a moment. Then Doug's father said, "Look, you can't let it get you down."

"I know," Doug replied. "But it's been a long time since I felt this incompetent. And I'm not imagining the whole thing, believe me. Cynthia Speedwell, the division president who was on the hiring committee, gave me a really odd look when we were leaving the meeting. I wish I knew what she was thinking."

Doug's father's only comment was: "Well, why don't you ask her, for goodness' sake?"

Up in the Air

Doug arrived at the airport at about the same time as Cynthia and Ben, and, as luck would have it, Doug and Cynthia sat next to each other on the plane. They engaged in small talk about the joys of being stuck in traffic. Then the conversation stalled. Finally, Cynthia turned to Doug. "May I ask you an impertinent question?" she asked.

Doug smiled. "Absolutely."

"Why are you and Peter having so much trouble getting your act together?"

What Went Wrong at Captiva, and What Should Happen Next?

Four commentators offer their advice.

➤ Miki Tsusaka

Miki Tsusaka is a vice president and director of the Boston Consulting Group. She leads the firm's Consumer Goods and Retail Practice as well as its e-commerce area in New York.

There's plenty of blame to go around in this case. Let's start with Doug Yacubian. He should have known that there's no such thing as a transition honeymoon for a hired-hand COO. (Healthy companies rarely go outside to find senior talent.) No one expected him to go in on his first day and grab the reins of leadership. But he should have been reaching out and selling his ideas to all his new constituents: his direct reports, the division presidents, the board, the CEO, and the company as a whole. The crisis situations were, in fact, good opportunities for him to meet with customers and distributors to establish a new leadership role. Instead of lamenting to his father, he must take action.

Peter Tyler also shares responsibility for the board's grumblings. It's clear he's having a hard time giving his baby over to the care of a relative stranger. If he had really been interested in making the transition work, he should have communicated and clarified the new COO's role to the company as soon as he brought Doug on board. Now that Captiva has weathered its crises, Peter may be ready to give up control. But the transition won't be automatic; he'll have to take the lead to dissipate people's frustrations about Doug.

Peter and Doug have both made mistakes, but the senior management team and the board aren't blameless. It's a travesty that team members haven't talked to one another about this situation. Unfortunately, crises and poor feedback are often the norm in management, but that does not excuse the team's inaction. Everyone on the senior team, including Cynthia Speedwell, could have worked aggressively at the outset to define and discuss the new COO's role and his integration into the leadership position—but they didn't.

Now that the damage has been done, Cynthia can help get things back on track. She needs to listen to Doug first—and then she needs to listen to Peter. After those conversations, she can draw up a "Monday morning list" of what to do next. It should look something like this:

1. Explain to the CEO and the COO in a direct and nonjudgmental way how people in the company view the situation and why. She should be clear about her own mistakes in the process: "I'm guilty of not bringing this up sooner."

2. Get reactions from Peter and Doug. Does Doug understand why people don't appreciate his efforts? Does Peter understand why people are unhappy with his choice of COO? Does he want Doug's appointment to work? Does he believe it can work?

3. Meet with them together and create a short list of action steps for Peter and Doug. The first should be to communicate to the company the events of the year, the accomplishments and the process so far, and what the imperatives are going forward. The list should emphasize tangible goals and a commitment to communication and feedback. If Peter and Doug can't agree on how to proceed—or if it seems that Peter has lost faith in Doug's abilities—Cynthia may want to help the CEO choose between giving the COO a limited period to exert his leadership and cutting his losses immediately by parting ways with him.

4. Broaden the discussion to include the management team. Cynthia should work with Doug and Peter to create a frank forum for conversation. The team must answer several questions: What will the relationship be between the COO and the CEO? How will the COO work with the division presidents? How will the leadership team evolve? Who will arbitrate if opinions differ? How will the responsibilities of Captiva's change initiatives be divided? Afterward, the team needs to deliver a clear, positive message to the board.

5. Point out to Peter that the CEO is ultimately responsible for ensuring that the coming year isn't a repeat of the previous one. He needs to express confidence before the board so that he and the other senior managers aren't blindsided at another meeting.

If Captiva's leaders can execute these steps, they'll clear up the confusion and mistrust that have steadily grown over the past year. They'll also put the company in a good position to transform itself yet again.

➤ Mark Smith

Mark Smith is a managing director of Korn/Ferry International, a global executive-recruiting firm. He leads the Boston office.

In this case, neither the board nor senior management was clear on objectives or what they were getting into. The CEO told Doug that the first year would be about learning the ropes and building relationships. Meanwhile, the board and other senior managers wanted results. But did they know what kind? Captiva has never had a COO. Some people thought that Doug would bring a bit of entrepreneurial flair with him from his days at BrewHeaven. But CEOs who are bringing in a second-in-command tend to want someone whose feet are on the ground—someone who slows the business down a bit and knows how to lay the bricks and spread the mortar. They do not want someone who is too slick or too fast.

The point is that Captiva's main stakeholders—the CEO, the board, and the management team—did not agree about what they expected from the new COO.

For his part, Doug may have made a serious career blunder. It seems to me that he has been seduced by largeness and complexity and has delusions of grandeur.

Doug's success at Marcella was likely a result of his old CEO's entrepreneurial abilities. I would guess that Jack Marcella was the driving force behind the business and that Doug was the implementer, not the creator. Because Captiva is a more complex business involving more product lines, he now has to do more than just follow someone else's plan.

The two businesses are quite different. I would guess that BrewHeaven is a little like Nantucket Nectars—it found a market, created a branded product, and built a business. The company has probably moved forward quickly without diverging from its course. Captiva, on the other hand, is an old company of established but varied lines that has to constantly reinvent itself rather than build itself from the ground up. Doug was probably not familiar with the level of complexity he encountered at Captiva.

This case is also about power. Even if you have the title of COO, you can't function without power, and there are only three ways to get it: you are given it and your mandate is clearly defined; you seize it through aggressiveness or a palace coup; or you get lucky and somebody dies or leaves. None of these happened in Doug's case.

After a shaky year and a tough board meeting, Doug is feeling defensive. He is losing confidence in himself, and the more he does that, the more he will feel that he's under attack.

What is the next step? The burden must fall on Doug. Turning things around is probably a long shot, but Doug should try. He can start by enlisting Cynthia's support for some of his projects as part of a general plan to build loyalty among a few key people. He may be able to do this by getting close to them and figuring out how he can help them.

Doug really needs a few clear, clean, immediate wins so he can say to the entire company, "Look what I've done." He has to be willing to take some risks: to ask for forgiveness, not permission. It may cost him his job, but it is the only way he can gain a lot of respect quickly—and not taking any risks is just as likely to cost him his job.

It is crucial that Doug get measurable results. Both sides must understand how and when his performance will be measured. In this case, the agreement might have been,

"Within 12 months of joining Captiva as COO, I will accomplish the following five things [the five then would be listed] . . . ; I will have the resources, budget, and people I need to carry them out; and 50% of my compensation will depend on my accomplishing those objectives."

Doug may save himself if he can take credit for important wins. But it will be an uphill battle. In the meantime, I would counsel him to start thinking about career alternatives.

➤ Fred K. Foulkes

Fred K. Foulkes is a professor of management policy and the director of the Human Resources Policy Institute at Boston University's School of Management.

The problem here is that it's unclear what any of the parties really wants. And because the clock has been ticking for a year now, it falls on Doug to figure out—fast—what the CEO wants, what the division presidents expect, and what he can deliver.

Start with Peter Tyler. We don't know what he really thinks. He may feel that Doug's doing a great job as he slowly learns the ropes. Or he may be patiently waiting for him to show more initiative. Another possibility is that he doesn't want a COO around at all. The board may have put pressure on him to hire someone, and he may have agreed only to keep the board happy. In reality, he may want to be involved in every decision and may want everyone reporting to him.

The division heads' response to the new COO has also been ambiguous. Ben Esperanza and Cynthia Speedwell are critical of Doug for "folding his tent" too early. But they seem to see him as a peer, not as their boss. And because he doesn't appear to command authority, the division heads are going to say, "I don't know where this guy is coming from, but his suggestions won't work in my division. So let him muck around someplace else!" But they may really need someone who can influence the CEO on their behalf.

Doug is perhaps the most curious character of all. It's unclear how the COO job fits his interests. He has little chance of succeeding Peter, so where does he go from here? Is this the end of his career? It's unlikely that he would want to become a division president.

A coach can be very useful when a company brings in a high-level person from the outside. Such an individual, hired by human resources but selected by the person who is being helped, can provide the new hire with feedback and help him work more effectively with his boss, his peers, and his subordinates. In the past, companies hired independent consultants to coach executives whose careers were in trouble. But in recent years, many organizations have begun employing outside coaches to help high-level transitions run more smoothly.

Doug is sharing his frustration with his father. He should also be listening and talking to Cynthia, the other division presidents, and the CEO. A heart-to-heart with his boss is critical at this point. One other route would be to talk to some of the impatient board members. But that would be very risky because it might reflect negatively on Peter. That's really a last resort.

Every person in Doug's situation has a honeymoon that lasts maybe three to six months. Then people start asking, "What's he really doing? How is he contributing?" After a year to 18 months, they often conclude, "Well, it wasn't a good match; it didn't work out. The person didn't fit our culture." And they have to get rid of the person. Doug's in danger of meeting that fate. To avert it, he'll have to find out what Peter's really thinking, and he'll have to build some strong relationships with the division heads. He'll need to get results—show people that he has some value to add to the company. And he'll have to look at himself in the mirror and decide what he really wants and why he took the job at Captiva in the first place.

➤ George Hornig

George Hornig is a private investor. Most recently he was executive vice president of Deutsche Bank Americas Holding Corporation. He is based in New York.

When a guy like Doug comes in as the number two, he has to focus on one thing: building a relationship with the CEO. That's an art. The CEO has to be comfortable with the new guy, but he also has to understand that, like it or not, he's got to allow the COO to take initiatives and run with them.

Peter and Doug missed an opportunity during the product recall. Doug came up with some very good ideas, and Peter should have let him pursue them. Maybe Peter was right to be the one doing interviews with the trade press, because the CEO's is the most visible public face of most companies. But Peter could have given the COO the green light to visit the U.S. distributors. That would have given Doug a contribution to point to. When no green light appeared, Doug made the mistake of deciding not to push the matter.

He missed other opportunities, too. He could have taken on more responsibility during the panic surrounding fourth-quarter numbers. He could have gone to Peter and said, "Look, let me figure out how to deal with the impact of the recall and what we need to do to make the earnings targets. This is something I can and should handle." That would have been a great way for Doug to work with people all over the company and to establish himself across divisions.

That's exactly the role the COO should be playing. What the division leaders need is a COO who can solve problems—someone who has enough clout with the boss to get things done. And they need someone who can act as a filter between them and the CEO. Right now, the division heads can't see any value in having Doug on board. He's down to his last chance to get deeply into something or find an issue that is clearly his.

That issue could be the restructuring. The CEO probably wouldn't mind handing Doug this unpleasant job. If Doug takes it over and earns a reputation among the division presidents as someone who is fair and effective, he'll gain new allies. On the other hand, if he fails to win them over—and he certainly hasn't been aggressive enough in building relationships—they'll just ignore him and go straight to the CEO, and Doug will continue to drift like an unmoored buoy.

Doug's dilemma reminds me of something Lawrence Taylor said when he was being inducted into the Pro Football Hall of Fame: "The crime isn't falling down, it's not getting up after you've been knocked down." The COO's been knocked down, and it remains to be seen whether he'll be able to pull himself up.

He could definitely use some help from Peter. The CEO seems reluctant to engage with the new guy; maybe he's afraid to give up power. But Peter has to get it through his head that he can still be the public face of Captiva while letting someone else handle the day-to-day stuff. That's what the company needs, and that's what Doug was hired to do. Peter has to say to the company, "This is my guy; listen to him and work with him."

Originally published in November–December 1999

Reprint 99606

ABOUT THE CONTRIBUTORS

Julia Kirby is a senior editor at HBR.

Steve Kerr is the chief learning officer at Goldman Sachs in New York. Prior to joining Goldman Sachs in 2001, he spent seven years as the chief learning officer and head of leadership development at GE. He was responsible for GE's leadership development center at Crotonville.

Eric McNulty is the managing director of the conferences division of Harvard Business School Publishing, HBR's parent company, in Boston.

Diane L. Coutu is a senior editor at HBR.

Sarah Cliffe is a senior editor at HBR.

Robert Galford consults with senior managers on performance, organizational, and career issues. He also teaches in executive education programs for professional services firms and at Northwestern University's Kellogg Graduate School of Management. He lives in Concord, Massachusetts.

Harvard Business Review Paperback Series

The Harvard Business Review Paperback Series offers the best thinking on cutting-edge management ideas from the world's leading thinkers, researchers, and managers. Designed for leaders who believe in the power of ideas to change business, these books will be useful to managers at all levels of experience, but especially senior executives and general managers. In addition, this series is widely used in training and executive development programs.

Books are priced at $19.95 U.S.
Price subject to change.

Title	Product #
Harvard Business Review **Interviews with CEOs**	3294
Harvard Business Review on **Advances in Strategy**	8032
Harvard Business Review on **Becoming a High Performance Manager**	1296
Harvard Business Review on **Brand Management**	1445
Harvard Business Review on **Breakthrough Leadership**	8059
Harvard Business Review on **Breakthrough Thinking**	181X
Harvard Business Review on **Building Personal and Organizational Resilience**	2721
Harvard Business Review on **Business and the Environment**	2336
Harvard Business Review on **Change**	8842
Harvard Business Review on **Compensation**	701X
Harvard Business Review on **Corporate Ethics**	273X
Harvard Business Review on **Corporate Governance**	2379
Harvard Business Review on **Corporate Responsibility**	2748
Harvard Business Review on **Corporate Strategy**	1429
Harvard Business Review on **Crisis Management**	2352
Harvard Business Review on **Culture and Change**	8369
Harvard Business Review on **Customer Relationship Management**	6994
Harvard Business Review on **Decision Making**	5572
Harvard Business Review on **Effective Communication**	1437

To order, call 1-800-668-6780, or go online at www.HBSPress.org

Title	Product #
Harvard Business Review on **Entrepreneurship**	9105
Harvard Business Review on **Finding and Keeping the Best People**	5564
Harvard Business Review on **Innovation**	6145
Harvard Business Review on **Knowledge Management**	8818
Harvard Business Review on **Leadership**	8834
Harvard Business Review on **Leadership at the Top**	2756
Harvard Business Review on **Leading in Turbulent Times**	1806
Harvard Business Review on **Managing Diversity**	7001
Harvard Business Review on **Managing High-Tech Industries**	1828
Harvard Business Review on **Managing People**	9075
Harvard Business Review on **Managing the Value Chain**	2344
Harvard Business Review on **Managing Uncertainty**	9083
Harvard Business Review on **Managing Your Career**	1318
Harvard Business Review on **Marketing**	8040
Harvard Business Review on **Measuring Corporate Performance**	8826
Harvard Business Review on **Mergers and Acquisitions**	5556
Harvard Business Review on **Motivating People**	1326
Harvard Business Review on **Negotiation**	2360
Harvard Business Review on **Nonprofits**	9091
Harvard Business Review on **Organizational Learning**	6153
Harvard Business Review on **Strategic Alliances**	1334
Harvard Business Review on **Strategies for Growth**	8850
Harvard Business Review on **The Business Value of IT**	9121
Harvard Business Review on **The Innovative Enterprise**	130X
Harvard Business Review on **Turnarounds**	6366
Harvard Business Review on **What Makes a Leader**	6374
Harvard Business Review on **Work and Life Balance**	3286

Harvard Business Essentials

In the fast-paced world of business today, everyone needs a personal resource—a place to go for advice, coaching, background information, or answers. The Harvard Business Essentials series fits the bill. Concise and straightforward, these books provide highly practical advice for readers at all levels of experience. Whether you are a new manager interested in expanding your skills or an experienced executive looking to stay on top, these solution-oriented books give you the reliable tips and tools you need to improve your performance and get the job done. Harvard Business Essentials titles will quickly become your constant companions and trusted guides.

These books are priced at $19.95 U.S., except as noted.
Price subject to change.

Title	Product #
Harvard Business Essentials: **Negotiation**	1113
Harvard Business Essentials: **Managing Creativity and Innovation**	1121
Harvard Business Essentials: **Managing Change and Transition**	8741
Harvard Business Essentials: **Hiring and Keeping the Best People**	875X
Harvard Business Essentials: **Finance**	8768
Harvard Business Essentials: **Business Communication**	113X
Harvard Business Essentials: **Manager's Toolkit ($24.95)**	2896
Harvard Business Essentials: **Managing Projects Large and Small**	3213
Harvard Business Essentials: **Creating Teams with an Edge**	290X

To order, call 1-800-668-6780, or go online at www.HBSPress.org

The Results-Driven Manager

The Results-Driven Manager series collects timely articles from *Harvard Management Update* and *Harvard Management Communication Letter* to help senior to middle managers sharpen their skills, increase their effectiveness, and gain a competitive edge. Presented in a concise, accessible format to save managers valuable time, these books offer authoritative insights and techniques for improving job performance and achieving immediate results.

These books are priced at $14.95 U.S.
Price subject to change.

Title	Product #
The Results-Driven Manager: **Face-to-Face Communications for Clarity and Impact**	3477
The Results-Driven Manager: **Managing Yourself for the Career You Want**	3469
The Results-Driven Manager: **Presentations That Persuade and Motivate**	3493
The Results-Driven Manager: **Teams That Click**	3507
The Results-Driven Manager: **Winning Negotiations That Preserve Relationships**	3485

Management Dilemmas:
Case Studies from the Pages of
Harvard Business Review

How often do you wish you could turn to a panel of experts to guide you through tough management situations? The Management Dilemmas series provides just that. Drawn from the pages of *Harvard Business Review*, each insightful volume poses several perplexing predicaments and shares the problem-solving wisdom of leading experts. Engagingly written, these solutions-oriented collections help managers make sound judgment calls when addressing everyday management dilemmas.

These books are priced at $19.95 U.S.
Price subject to change.

Title	Product #
Management Dilemmas: **When Change Comes Undone**	5038
Management Dilemmas: **When Good People Behave Badly**	5046
Management Dilemmas: **When Marketing Becomes a Minefield**	290X

To order, call 1-800-668-6780, or go online at www.HBSPress.org

Readers of the Management Dilemmas series find the following Harvard Business School Press books of interest.

If you find these books useful:	You may also like these:
When Change Comes Undone	Leading Change (7471) The Heart of Change (2549)
When Good People Behave Badly	Toxic Emotions at Work (2573) The Set-Up-to-Fail Syndrome (9490)
When Marketing Becomes a Minefield	How Customers Think (8261) Marketing Moves (6005) United We Brand (7982)

How to Order

Harvard Business School Press publications are available worldwide
from your local bookseller or online retailer.
You can also call

1-800-668-6780

Our product consultants are available to help you
8:00 a.m.–6:00 p.m., Monday–Friday, Eastern Time.
Outside the U.S. and Canada, call: 617-783-7450
Please call about special discounts for quantities greater than ten.

You can order online at

www.HBSPress.org